HOSPITALITY
—the sacred art

ALSO AVAILABLE IN
THE ART OF SPIRITUAL LIVING SERIES

Running—The Sacred Art:
Preparing to Practice
by Dr. Warren A. Kay
Foreword by Kristin Armstrong

Giving—The Sacred Art:
Creating a Lifestyle of Generosity
by Lauren Tyler Wright

Thanking and Blessing—The Sacred Art:
Spiritual Vitality through Gratefulness
by Jay Marshall, PhD
Foreword by Philip Gulley

Everyday Herbs in Spiritual Life:
A Guide to Many Practices
written and illustrated by Michael J. Caduto

The Sacred Art of Fasting:
Preparing to Practice
by Thomas Ryan, CSP

The Sacred Art of Bowing:
Preparing to Practice
by Andi Young

The Sacred Art of Chant:
Preparing to Practice
by Ana Hernández

The Sacred Art of Lovingkindness:
Preparing to Practice
by Rabbi Rami Shapiro
Foreword by Marcia Ford

Discovering the
Hidden Spiritual Power
of Invitation and Welcome

HOSPITALITY
—the sacred art

REV. NANETTE SAWYER
FOREWORD BY REV. DIRK FICCA

Walking Together, Finding the Way®
SKYLIGHT PATHS®
PUBLISHING
Woodstock, Vermont

Hospitality—The Sacred Art
Discovering the Hidden Spiritual Power of Invitation and Welcome

2008 First Printing
© 2008 by Nanette Sawyer

For information regarding permission to reprint material from this book, please mail or fax your request in writing to SkyLight Paths Publishing, Permissions Department, at the address / fax number listed below, or e-mail your request to permissions@skylightpaths.com.

Library of Congress Cataloging-in-Publication Data
Sawyer, Nanette.
  Hospitality, the sacred art : discovering the hidden spiritual power of invitation and welcome / by Nanette Sawyer.
      p. cm.—(The art of spiritual living)
  Includes bibliographical references and index.
  ISBN-13: 978-1-59473-228-7 (pbk.)
  ISBN-10: 1-59473-228-0 (pbk.)
  1. Hospitality. 2. Generosity. 3. Hospitality—Religious aspects. 4. Generosity—Religious aspects. 5. Spiritual life. I. Title.
  BJ2021.S29 2007
  241'.671—dc22

                                                        2007037104

10   9   8   7   6   5   4   3   2   1

SkyLight Paths Publishing is creating a place where people of different spiritual traditions come together for challenge and inspiration, a place where we can help each other understand the mystery that lies at the heart of our existence.

SkyLight Paths sees both believers and seekers as a community that increasingly transcends traditional boundaries of religion and denomination—people wanting to learn from each other, *walking together, finding the way.*

Manufactured in the United States of America
Cover design: Jenny Buono
SkyLight Paths, "Walking Together, Finding the Way," and colophon are trademarks of LongHill Partners, Inc., registered in the U.S. Patent and Trademark Office.

Walking Together, Finding the Way®
Published by SkyLight Paths Publishing
A Division of LongHill Partners, Inc.
Sunset Farm Offices, Route 4, P.O. Box 237
Woodstock, VT 05091
Tel: (802) 457-4000   Fax: (802) 457-4004
www.skylightpaths.com

This book is dedicated to
my mother and father,
who invited, welcomed, and nurtured me
into this world;
and
to you, the reader.
I wrote it for you.

CONTENTS

Foreword   ix
Introduction: Hospitality as Transformation   1

1   Hospitality to God: Welcoming God's Welcome   10

2   Hospitality to Self: Inviting the Authentic Self   30

3   Hospitality to Family: Offering Full Presence
     to Those Closest to Us   52

4   Hospitality to Neighbors: Becoming the Merciful
     Neighbor   72

5   Hospitality to Strangers: Pursuing Kinship
     Rather than Estrangement   94

6   Hospitality to Enemies: Extending
     Generosity through Non-Retaliation   118

7   Hospitality to Creation: Knowing
     Creation Relationally   142

Acknowledgments   167
Notes   169
Suggestions for Further Reading   176
Index of Exercises and Practices   180

FOREWORD

by Rev. Dirk Ficca

The act of hospitality—of welcoming the other, whoever the other is—is an imperative in many of the world's religious and spiritual traditions, in part because it can be a burden as well as a blessing, as Kathleen Norris observes in her book *Dakota: A Spiritual Geography*:

> Saint Benedict, writing in the sixth century, notes that a monastery is never without guests, and admonishes monks to "receive all guests as Christ." Monks have been quick to recognize that such hospitality, while undoubtedly a blessing, can also create burdens for them. A story said to originate in a Russian Orthodox monastery has an older monk telling a younger one: "I have finally learned to accept people as they are. Whatever they are in the world, a prostitute, a prime minister, it is all the same to me. But sometimes I see a stranger coming up the road and I say, 'Oh, Jesus Christ, is it you again?'"[1]

While extolling the spiritual virtues and personal benefits of a lifestyle of hospitality, Nanette Sawyer does not offer the typical platitudes and quick-fix promises that characterize so much of marketplace spirituality these days. In her generous and challenging exploration of the sacred art of hospitality, Sawyer squarely faces the reality that intentional hospitality is ultimately a matter of practice that calls for radical openness, self-discipline, and a willingness to be changed by an encounter with the other, be it a member of your family, your next door neighbor, a stranger, an enemy, the Earth, or God. Such challenges are why, perhaps, hospitality must at times be framed as an imperative. In her view, the practice of hospitality is religion and spirituality at their most sacred, and as demanding as any form of true art.

That hospitality is central to traditions as diverse as Buddhism, Christianity, Judaism, Hinduism, and Islam, to name a few, might come as a surprise to many who view religion as a principal source of misunderstanding, fanaticism, hatred, and conflict. All of these traditions have been historically, and are being currently, interpreted in ways that urge and guide their respective followers to be indifferently or aggressively inhospitable to each other. In a post-September 11th world, driven by the forces of globalization and religious identity, where communities of often starkly different languages, cultures, and traditions are now living side by side in major urban centers, the stakes have never been higher for a different reading of these traditions, with hospitality as the guiding principle. Hospitality as a defining mark of identity for individuals, communities, and cultures is a necessity if the world is going to come to grips with diversity in sane and life-affirming ways.

In making her case, Sawyer both describes and models what she is proposing about the practice of hospitality. She writes as a Christian, but draws on the wisdom and experience of a variety of perspectives in creative ways that will be helpful to a broad spectrum of inquirers, from those committed to a particular tradition to those who might call themselves seekers. Her central concepts of *receptivity*, *reverence*, and *generosity* are easy to grasp and yet profoundly useful for plumbing the depths of what she calls transformative spiritual hospitality. And she has firsthand experience in the practice, both on the receiving and giving ends. Stories from her own life, and from the lives of others, illuminate the processes, the pitfalls, and the practical dimensions of this sacred art.

In the end, it is this practicality, the "groundedness," of her approach that I appreciate the most. While there is rock-solid scholarship and a carefully reasoned foundation to her rationale, Sawyer has been true to the notion that hospitality is finally not a philosophical stance or a theological concept but a matter of practice that must be lived out. I remember hearing a story about the renowned Catholic theologian Karl Rahner—who was German and whose writings no one would call highly accessible—sitting beside a podium as someone read his lecture to the audience in English, and praying the rosary. Apparently no matter how complex or lofty his thoughts, for Rahner they were not to be confused with, or a substitute for, spiritual practice, for the actual living out of his convictions.

As an innovative pastor and pioneer in forging a new path to authentic spirituality in a religiously diverse world, Sawyer has provided us with a multitude of ways to engage in the practice of hospitality, from prayer and meditation to conversation, friendship, and service. There are descriptions and exercises to be done to initiate or enhance your own practice. Questions to ponder that will lead to further reading and new experiences. Advice on how to engage with intentional communities of faith and action. Work to be done that will improve the world.

Sawyer trusts the practice of hospitality. She trusts that as people embark on the practice it will teach and guide and transform them in ways that she doesn't feel the need to program or predict. If you are freely persuaded, then you will embark on the journey. If you undertake the journey with a commitment to see it through, you will be changed. If hospitality grows as an imperative for religious and spiritual communities, there will be new hope for the world. Sawyer invites you to give it a try, see where it takes you. She offers insights and encouragement as a companion for your journey. What could be more hospitable than that?

INTRODUCTION:

HOSPITALITY AS

TRANSFORMATION

This book is about transformation through the spiritual practice of deep hospitality. Becoming a person of hospitality will both center you and open you up; it will help you know yourself better, as well as perceive the richness of creation more fully. I call this kind of hospitality *deep* because it comes from our inner core and has the capacity to significantly change our self-understanding as well as the quality of all our relationships. This capacity for change is why I also call it transformative spiritual hospitality. It is centered in our understanding about who we are and how we are related to that which is holy.

Transformative spiritual hospitality, as we shall see, flows from *receptivity, reverence,* and *generosity*—three qualities that reflect a basic pattern of movement: *in-with-out.* Becoming receptive is preparing ourselves to be able to invite others into our lives, our hearts, and sometimes our homes; it is the development of an *inner* state. Reverence is a state of *being with* others, honoring and welcoming them while generosity reflects a *flowing out* of physical, emotional, and spiritual care. In certain chapters I use the related concepts—awareness, acceptance, and action—to explore methods for practicing the qualities of receptivity, reverence, and generosity in our lives. Developing your capacity to embody these qualities will help you discover the spiritual power of hospitality and will bring you closer to God, yourself, and the world.

This is a spiritual as well as a practical book, filled with insights from scriptures, spiritual practitioners, and thinkers from around the world. It's full of exercises and experiments that you can do to discover the natural sources of hospitality deep within you. It reflects my own efforts to integrate my studies in comparative world religions with my spiritual practices. As a Christian, the teachings of Jesus have been illuminated for me by the words of Mahatma Gandhi, the philosophy of Martin Buber, and the practices of Thich Nhat Hanh, as much as by the teachings of Martin Luther King Jr.—you'll see that this book is influenced by all of them and many more.

But why *hospitality*? I mentioned to a friend of mine that I was working on this book and he got a befuddled look on his face. You know the one—eyebrows raised and drawn together, lips pursed ever so slightly, holding a tiny question. How could you fill a whole book on the topic of hospitality? "Be nice to people when they're at your house." Doesn't that about cover it? Use pretty place mats with color-coordinated napkins and an attractive centerpiece involving candles and a seasonally appropriate flower or twig. Right? Entertaining—that's what hospitality is, isn't it?

Nope. That's why this book is not about how to throw better dinner parties. Although dinner might be part of hospitality, this book is really about the inner quality of our own spirits and how hospitality can transform our relationship with the world.

HOSPITALITY CHANGES US

There have been people in my life who have astonished me with their generosity. They seemed to make their hearts available to me in ways that caused my own heart to open. In times when I was struggling financially and personally, they extended to me a simple acceptance and deep respect, which allowed me to step into and acknowledge my own vulnerability and accept the hospitality they offered.

The ways people extended hospitality to me in times of need shook me and changed me: when I was broke and couldn't afford a car, and people loaned me theirs; when a devastating life change left me with no place to live and a friend took me in, sacrificing to me her newly renovated writing studio to be my home for a year; when an acquaintance invited me to house-sit for her and she told me, "Have a party while you're here, invite your friends, have a barbecue, eat anything we have." The generosity inherent in this last example was startling to me. I was so astonished by the wild permission-giving nature of that attitude that I felt my being relax. I vowed to make that same offer to someone else when I had the means. Their hospitality changed me!

In fact, there came a time when I was able to welcome a friend into my own place, as I had been welcomed at other times. I told her, "Have a party while you're here, invite your friends. Let this be your home while you're here." Having been so warmly and compassionately received by others, I myself was transformed. I was able to relax into my own confident openness and, in turn, extend hospitality with love and generosity.

What I experienced in the graciousness of others was a simple and sincere generosity. It was a deep hospitality, offered authentically and respectfully. They approached me with hands open, not fists clenched, and I saw how beautiful that was. It generated in me a deep gratitude and gave me an experience of grace. In turn, I wanted to embody that grace and reflect that beauty. Receiving deep hospitality changes us; learning to offer it changes us even more.

HOSPITALITY REFLECTS OUR POSTURE TOWARD LIFE

The practice of deep hospitality can help us step into a more vital, vibrant embrace of this great adventure we call life—which includes our relationship with God, however you might define God. We'll take a closer look at our language about God in chapter 1. But, however we conceive of God or understand the nature of Ultimate Reality—whether it is as Creator, Interbeing, Emptiness, Consciousness, or Life Itself—we have choices to make about the inner posture we hold in relationship to that reality. We have the power to become aware and to choose how we will act in our lives. This book is an invitation to walk through life with a liberating posture of receptivity, reverence, and generosity.

The practice of hospitality begins with *receptivity*, which is fundamentally a *posture of invitation*; it's the impulse of openness and possibility that initiates acts of hospitality. Receptivity is not about "receiving" something so much as it is about awareness, the kind of full awareness that allows us to perceive ourselves and each other accurately. It is an inward state that invites others into our lives. Receptivity will allow your relationships to flourish in newer, deeper ways than you thought possible.

The next step in the process of hospitality is *reverence*, which is a *posture of welcome*; it exists in the space between people, where we hold each other with honor and respect. To welcome deeply means to encounter the fullness of a person, perceive his or her inherent integrity and intrinsic value, and then engage it with your full self. Reverence says, I value who you are and what you have to offer to me, to us (you and me), and to the world. In a state of reverence, we stand in the full presence of another, while being fully present ourselves. There is deep acceptance and love in this state, as we encounter the image of God in each other.

The completion of the circle of hospitality is *generosity*. Generosity is a *posture of nurture*; it transforms invitation and welcome into a complete expression of hospitality. It is an outflow of physical, spiritual, and emotional care and gratitude, the actions we take to express compassionate love and grace. Generosity changes us by affirming the abundance of life itself.

This abundance is not related to how many possessions we have; rather, it's about living life in all its fullness—*abundant life*. Suddenly, we realize that we have much more than we understood ourselves to have. We begin to realize that what we actually *need* in human life is a lot less stuff and a lot more relationship.

This book will introduce you to ideas and practices that can help you hold a receptive, reverent, and generous posture toward life, love, God, reality, other people, and creation itself. The ideas here reflect my own adventures with life and my journey toward hospitality. In chapter 1, I write at length about a spiritual experience I had with hospitality that deeply changed me. It happened in a church, which was surprising because I had been disenfranchised from the faith of my youth for many years. Yet, I had remained deeply interested in spiritual life. I had gone to Harvard Divinity School to study comparative world religions, and while I was studying there I met a few people who did go to church. One of them, a dear friend, invited me to his church, where I had a profound experience of the radical hospitality of Jesus in the ritual moment of communion. After that, I started showing up more at that church, and the members welcomed me and embodied the spirit of love in their ministry the way I imagined Jesus did in his. Experiencing that love changed my life.

In that small church in South Boston I felt my call to the ministry based on a deep desire to share the radical, Jesus-inspired hospitality that I learned there. So I went to seminary and was ordained in the Presbyterian Church (USA). Now I'm the pastor at a young new church that meets in an art gallery on the west side of Chicago. We're called Wicker Park Grace (Wicker Park is our neighborhood), and an important part of our identity as a community is shaped by that word *grace*. Grace is something we've experienced from each other, and which we're always learning how to extend. It's about offering friendliness and friendship, kindness and warmth. It's about pushing through our fears and timidities in order to welcome others.

Sometimes it's also about being quiet enough long enough to really be able to hear the stories and wisdom that others can bring us.

I write as a Christian, but these concepts related to hospitality are available to you whatever religious or spiritual path you follow, or none at all. Grace, for example, like hospitality, is about extending invitations and caring sincerely about the people we encounter. Grace is something that the divine presence, which I usually refer to as God, offers to us all the time—an unconditional love that affirms how precious each human being is. This grace of God is a deep welcome, an existential embrace, a holy hospitality that fills us up. Extending hospitality *to* God means welcoming this embrace until we can't help *offering* it as well.

HOSPITALITY AS PRACTICE

At Wicker Park Grace, we have been experimenting with the practice of hospitality in a number of creative ways. As a new church, we've been trying some innovative things, such as having a changing pattern in our regular Sunday gatherings. Two Sundays a month we do something prayerful, usually a vespers gathering (which is prayer in the late afternoon), and the other two Sundays a month we share a meal and discuss various topics. We did this on purpose, because we wanted to have a lot of time together to get to know each other, and we figured what better way than to eat and talk? This is one of the ways that we built hospitality into the actual structure of our lives together.

Hospitality, we knew, included sitting at table together, being friendly, and growing more connected by getting to know each other and by spending time together. However, it turns out that hospitality is a little harder and a little deeper than we first imagined. Although we were eating and talking together, we noticed that we had a tendency to slip into our habits of superficiality. When greeting each other with, "How are you?" we habitually replied that we were good, fine. We didn't know how to engage each other in deeper conversation, or how to share our own lives and vulnerabilities with each other. Even though we had set aside so much time and space to be in community and to extend hospitality to each other, we found that we didn't really know how to do it! It turned out to be something that we actually needed to work on and think about and talk about and practice.

This surprised us, and it may surprise you as you read this book to discover that hospitality is a deeply spiritual practice that changes us the more we practice it. This book delves into some of the questions we began to think about as a community, including:

- How do we break out of our shyness or our intimidation around people we don't know?
- What keeps some people talking all the time and others quiet?
- How can we change that dynamic?
- How can we start a conversation that actually leads to people feeling closer afterward, and not just the same or, worse, *less* connected than they were before the conversation?
- How can we encourage each other to take the risks required to show our real human vulnerability in order to grow personally and become closer communally?
- What prevents us from making the commitment to consistently showing up in order to be together?
- Why are we hesitant to invite people into our homes?

In some ways, all these questions boil down to *how can we be truly hospitable?* And why should we be? Why is it important? This book gives some food for thought as well as some hands-on and hearts-open practices to help us dig into these and many related questions.

CIRCLES OF HOSPITALITY

Since hospitality both affects and reflects our spiritual wholeness, this book explores hospitality going out from our center in all directions in ever-widening circles of relationship. Hospitality begins in our spiritual core, and so chapter 1 explores hospitality to God, while opening up new ways of thinking of God as the matrix of life itself. Hospitality to God means being open to sacredness and the interconnected nature of God, self, and creation. Chapter 2 then goes into practices that can help us love and accept ourselves, to heal and discover a deeper, broader, bigger self than we knew we were. Extending hospitality to the self means beginning to practice the three elements of hospitality—receptivity, reverence, and generosity—toward ourselves. In doing this, we discover that the true self is deeply interconnected with divinity, with God—a connection that gives us energy and courage to engage in acts of hospitality with resources from a source greater than ourselves. Chapter 3 broadens the circle of hospitality to the family and to places where we experience the special joys and challenges of intimacy of all sorts. Offering hospitality here will help us create a safe and generous home in which our lives can be nurtured and from which we can offer gracious hospitality to others.

From there, we look in chapter 4 at neighbors—what *is* a neighbor and how to be one—how to reach out in friendship and generosity. We explore the interconnectedness of life as expressed in the concept of interbeing, and consider ways to "dwell in nearness" to one another. Chapter 5 takes a look at the alienation we can reinforce by seeing people as "strangers." This chapter is an invitation to pursue kinship rather than estrangement, and includes suggested practices for dealing with fear, pridefulness, and shame—emotions that tend to increase estrangement. Chapter 6 reaches into the difficult topic of loving our enemies. How might we extend hospitality even in the face of hostility? With suggestions from Martin Luther King Jr., this chapter explores the ideas of non-retaliation and active nonviolence. We also look into some of Mahatma Gandhi's ideas about "soul force," or *satyagraha*, as well as the importance of claiming our personal power for right action in relationships. Chapter 7 brings us full circle back to God and the matrix of life through an exploration of hospitality to creation as encountered in both urban and rural settings.

My own spiritual journey has truly been one of *walking together, finding the way*, as the motto of SkyLight Paths Publishing suggests. It has been a process of extending hospitality to an abundance of ideas and perspectives about God, life, and religious and spiritual practice—which has truly illuminated my path. I needed to do this for my own development of spiritual practice, and it's another example of how receptivity, reverence, and generosity can transform us. Through this practice of hospitality to ideas and the people who hold them, I have been opened and inspired, nurtured and reassured of the deep relationality that is life. I hope that my learnings can shine a light on your path as well.

CHAPTER ONE

HOSPITALITY TO GOD

Welcoming God's Welcome

The weather was so dramatic today that I cleared all the plants off my broad windowsill and crawled up there, sitting knees to chest, so that I could have a front row seat at the tremendous show of power. It was a thunderstorm, the wind whipping the trees into a frenzy and breaking the raindrops into such small particles that it looked like an all-pervasive mist being flung back heavenward. But it was pouring, not misting, and the lightning turned the sky yellow, then gray, then yellow again. People parked their cars on the city street below and ran for the shelter of nearby buildings.

As I watched this scene of nature's power and human life unfolding outside my window, the words of thirteenth-century mystic Meister Eckhart came to mind. Eckhart said that God's very being saturated all of life itself: "God's being is my life ..." he wrote. "God's is-ness is my is-ness, and neither more nor less."[1] Twelfth-century abbess and mystic Hildegard of Bingen reflected on this same interconnectedness of God and life when she wrote, "God is life, that nurtures every creature in its kind."[2]

In another poem she addresses God as the life of the life of all creation, and goes on to say, "O current of power permeating all ... you bind and gather all ... together. Out of you clouds come streaming, winds take wing from you, dashing rain against stone; and ever-fresh springs well from you, washing the ever-green globe."[3] But sitting in my window, gazing down at people rushing along the sidewalk holding newspapers over their heads in a vain attempt to stay dry, I wondered, Where is God in *this*?

I was reaching for a bigger awareness of divine power and presence than we generally do from day to day. Words can't really convey the majesty and mystery of this vast and powerful God. The very word *God* is sometimes so overlaid with limiting concepts that it is difficult to get beyond the word to an authentic awareness of a real sacred presence in daily life.[4] So I asked myself questions in an effort to open my mind.

Is God the Force in the wind? Is God the Green in the leaves of the tree just a few feet from my window seat? Is God the Life in the rain pouring into the thirsty roots of all the plants and trees? I was inspired to take this train of thought by Hildegard of Bingen's poetry. The idea that God *is* life, the Life of the life of all living things, will be a key to the practice of hospitality we'll be exploring in this book.

However we think of or talk about God—as Creator, Life, fire of the Holy Spirit, is-ness, the "big I" (a concept we will explore shortly), or one of a million ways not mentioned here—we have choices about how to relate to or turn away from this matrix of our being. Choosing to be hospitable by practicing receptivity, reverence, and generosity in this essential relationship leads us into an abundant and vibrant life in which we become filled with love and compassion.

In a lesson called "God Giving," Zen master Shunryu Suzuki teaches that "according to Christianity, every existence in nature is something which was created for or given to us by God. This is the perfect idea of giving. But if you think that God created man, and that you are somehow separate from God, you are liable to think that you have the ability to create something separate, something not given by Him."[5] Suzuki differentiates between the "small I" and the "big I" in this teaching. The "small I" thinks that it is responsible for creating things and doing things all on its own—it forgets the power of God that is behind all creating, all doing. The "big I," by contrast, understands and remembers the interconnectedness of all things. It is the "big I" who creates and who gives. This is the "I" that is deeply connected to and interdependent on God. So all creation, all giving, and I would even say all hospitality, comes from this "big I," which is the power and being of God.

Buddhists don't usually use this "God" language, and Christians don't usually refer to God as "is-ness" as Meister Eckhart did. But I think that both are trying to describe the deep interconnectedness of all things, and the interpenetration of the power of creation with that which is created. I hear reverberations of St. Paul saying in the Book of Acts that God is the one in whom "we live and move and have our being."[6] Speaking of God is difficult because God is so much more than any word or concept can ever convey, and many people find that even referring to "God" at all is too limiting. Nevertheless, we speak, we wonder, we think, we share our musings with one another, and we tell the stories of our lives, seeking to understand more and to learn from one another's experiences.

Here's one story from my own life that was a big turning point in my experience of extending hospitality toward God, as well as a breakthrough in receiving God's hospitality toward me. It demonstrates how the three qualities of deep hospitality—receptivity, reverence, and generosity—work together.

RECEPTIVITY: OPENING THE DOOR TO GOD
Although I was raised Christian, I had a fairly negative experience in church as a child and stopped going as soon as I was old

enough to make that decision and my parents would let me get away with it. The sad thing is that I had not learned in church about God's love and real presence. We sang the song "Jesus loves the little children, all the children of the world," but it never felt true, and the people there didn't seem to embody that ideal. I felt judged, like I was not good enough, like I was not truly loved or accepted as I was. So I hadn't gone to church for a long time, and then one day a friend invited me to go to his church during Lent for a Wednesday-night prayer service.

At the time, I didn't really know what Lent was. I was just learning that it includes the six weeks leading up to Easter, during which Christians practice increased contemplation and focused spiritual practices to prepare themselves for a full and rich experience of Easter celebrations. When he invited me, my friend said, "Oh, yeah, we'll be having communion there."

That was another problem. I had never had communion. When I was a child, my mother told me not to take communion because I wasn't ready for it. I had no idea what "ready" meant, but I got the idea that something terrible would happen to me if I took some of the bread. This bread was not for me. I knew it was a pretty important ritual at church, and I had seen the trays of bread passed down aisles and through rows of people, everybody taking a piece. Similarly, trays filled with little tea-party doll-size cups of grape juice were passed along and everybody took his or her serving. I watched the silver trays go by.

Since then I had been taught that communion was only for people who believed certain things about Jesus, and I was pretty sure I didn't believe the right things. And, like I said, I hadn't been to church for a long time. So when my friend asked me to go to his church and the communion service, I said, "I don't think I would be invited to that." He looked right back at me and said, "I'm inviting you."

Well. That was a direct contradiction to my feelings and I had to reorganize all my insides to accept that. Looking back into his eyes, I had to allow myself to be invited. That was my first step in expressing my receptivity to God at that time. My friend was inviting me to Jesus' table, and I had to release the clenching of my heart in order to go through the doors of the church, doors I had closed a long time ago. Who was welcoming whom there? My friend was opening a door by inviting me, but I had to open another door in order to accept. I had to let go of some of my past experiences and beliefs in order to allow myself out of my past way of seeing things. I began to hold a more invitational posture; in this case, I was inviting a new experience of God in a place I didn't expect—church. This kind of invitation is the beginning of receptivity.

Vietnamese Buddhist monk and Zen master Thich Nhat Hanh says that there are special doors that allow us "to enter the realm of mindfulness, loving-kindness, peace, and joy." The Buddha is such a door: "a teacher who shows us the way in this life." Tradition holds that there are 84,000 doors of teaching, or Dharma doors, and Thich Nhat Hanh says that each one of us can open new Dharma doors "by our practice and our loving-kindness."[7] I think that this door in my heart that allowed me to receive my friend's invitation was door number 84,001. Opening it, I began a journey toward healing some childhood experiences of a very limited "God." I began to extend hospitality to God and was about to receive some transformational hospitality in return.

REVERENCE: ENTERING THE SPACE OF LOVE BETWEEN US

So I went with my friend to the little white clapboard church and entered through the bright red doors, feeling awkward, out of place, and tentative. I went as an alien, as a stranger, perhaps as a prodigal daughter, returning to a place that had once been home, uncertain of the welcome I would receive.

It was that time of day when twilight is just beginning to set in. The church sanctuary was dim and we were a small group, maybe eight people or so, sitting in the first couple of wooden pews and some folding chairs in a semicircle in front of the first pew. In this way we created a small circle. On the front white wall of the sanctuary, a large wooden cross seemed to hover in midair, suspended by some unseen means.

Everything felt strange there. Singing happened. Scripture was read. The pastor said a few words of reflection about the scripture. And then it was time for communion. Because we were a small group, we all got up and stood in a circle at the front of the church. After talking about communion a bit, the pastor walked around the circle, offering each person a loaf of bread from which to break off a chunk and a big shared cup of grape juice for each to dip the bread in.

It was mysterious and quiet. I felt a growing anxiety as he approached me. I had a lingering sensation of being unwelcome, of not belonging there, of being about to be rejected once again. The pastor stood in front of me and offered me the bread, "Nanette, the body of Christ, given for you." Why did I *believe* him? Suddenly, I heard these words as true.

For a moment I was transported to some mystical place, a table in another realm, where I was welcomed and loved. In this place, God wanted to feed and nourish me. As the bread was being passed to me and offered to me by name, I experienced a deep sensation of *with-ness*. It was a profound experience of a holy presence. I was with God and God was with me in the space between us, and all around us was an aura of compassionate love. The bread I broke and dipped and ate was not just flour, yeast, and water—it was a piece of *embrace*; it was the tenderest look a person could ever give or receive. Not just my mouth, and not just my heart, but my entire being seemed to open to receive this bread and to be *with* the holiness that was present.

This deep with-ness is the essence of reverence. Reverence is the quality of an encounter permeated with honor and com-passionate love. This is the second phase of transformative

spiritual hospitality, which grows out of the open space of receptivity and prepares the way for generous giving.

GENEROSITY: GIVING THE GIFTS THAT WE HAVE RECEIVED

There is a particularly cyclical quality of hospitality to God. In
my experience just described, I took an invitational posture
through receptivity and welcomed God's presence in reverence.
I made the initial movements of hospitality toward God, but the
completion of hospitality—generosity—I experienced profoundly as coming *from* God.

This is one of the unique qualities of hospitality to God. Once
we offer it to God, we also receive hospitality from God. After
that, we may find that the hospitality we offer to others is the hospitality that we have already received. People become agents of
God's love and God's hospitality. The love that touched me
through the communion experience, which I experienced as God's
love, was made real to me through the graciousness of other
human beings who invited me into their circle, offered me bread
and juice, and called me by name. Diana Butler Bass, researcher
and church scholar, describes the core practice of hospitality as
welcoming "strangers into the heart of God's transformative
love."[8] It was the invitation and welcome extended to me by my
friend and by his pastor (who later became my pastor) that
brought me to a place where I could have the more mystical experience of being welcomed into the heart of God's love. In effect,
they were sharing with me the experience of grace and hospitality
that they themselves had received.

Hospitality to God is circular in this way, because when we
welcome God we find that we ourselves are deeply welcomed into
God—into the life that "nurtures every creature" as Hildegard of
Bingen said. Whenever we open the door to this sacred source of
nurture, we have access to an unending supply of love. Eastern
Orthodox bishop Kallistos Ware describes this sort of holy love for

God and humans in this way: "By love, I don't mean merely an emotional feeling, but a fundamental attitude. In its deepest sense, love is the life, the energy, of God Himself in us."[9] Receiving this love-energy of God becomes a foundation for all our acts of hospitality as we seek to give what we have received. Jewish philosopher and theologian Martin Buber said that "God speaks to every man through the life which He gives him again and again. Therefore man can only answer God with the whole of life—with the way in which he lives this given life."[10]

Our "answer" to God's grace, love, and hospitality is expressed through our lives and our relationships. "Everything is waiting to be hallowed by you,"[11] Buber said. Theresa of Avila said that Jesus has no hands and feet on earth now, and so we must be his hands and feet. When human beings stand in for God, as we offer and receive on behalf of God with open hearts, God's grace can become suddenly, radically tangible. Similarly, Thich Nhat Hanh says that "without you, the Buddha is not real, it is just an idea. Without you, the Dharma cannot be practiced. It has to be practiced by someone.... That is why when we say, 'I take refuge in the Buddha,' we also hear, 'The Buddha takes refuge in me.'"[12]

If you are Buddhist, you can think about becoming the *Buddhakaya*, the body of the Buddha, and practicing compassion. If you are Christian, you can think about becoming the body of Christ, and offering the grace of God in a very real way. Then you can say, "It is no longer I who live, but it is Christ who lives in me."[13] Whatever your faith, or if you don't follow a traditional religious path at all, you can certainly still practice moving through life with a receptive, reverent, and generous spirit. This is entering into what Martin Buber called "the currents of universal reciprocity."[14]

PRACTICING RECEPTIVITY THROUGH CENTERING PRAYER

Let's begin to consider some exercises that can help us prepare to practice hospitality to God. The first and foundational step is developing a spirit of receptivity. One method of nurturing a receptive spirit is through a technique called Centering Prayer, which is a practice of holding an open, invitational posture toward God. Centering Prayer is also sometimes called the Prayer of Consent, because in Centering Prayer we are giving our consent for God to become active in us.

The practice is based on choosing a focal point as a symbol of your intention to welcome God's presence and action into your life. Many times this is a sacred word, but it could also be your breath or holding an inner posture of looking toward the divine presence. The sacred word you choose can be explicitly religious, based on your faith tradition, or it can be implicitly spiritual, expressing your intention of receptivity. So, for example, God, Spirit, Father, Mother, Mary, Jesus, on the one hand, or Love, Peace, Listen, Trust, Yes, on the other. My favorite word for this type of prayer is "Open," which I am able to hold in my mind without getting caught up in theological thoughts or questions.

Centering Prayer is a kind of meditation based on a book called *The Cloud of Unknowing*, written in the late fourteenth century by an anonymous author, possibly an English country priest or monk. It is based on the idea that God cannot be fully known or understood through our intellect or described adequately by words. The author even jokes about his inability to describe God, saying, "But now you will ask me, 'How am I to think of God himself, and what is he?' and I cannot answer you except to say 'I do not know!' For with this question you have brought me into the same darkness, the same cloud of unknowing where I want you to be!"[15] When you give up trying to talk about God and instead rest in receptivity, you have the possibility of directly encountering the mystery that we sometimes call "God."

In his book, *Open Mind, Open Heart*, Cistercian monk Thomas Keating describes the interior transformation that can occur through the practice of Centering Prayer. "One's way of seeing reality changes in the process. A restructuring of consciousness takes place which empowers one to perceive, relate and respond with increasing sensitivity to the divine presence in, through, and beyond everything that exists."[16] This kind of sensitivity to the divine presence will greatly enhance your ability to offer deep hospitality to God, to others, and even to creation. Below are Keating's steps for practicing Centering Prayer, which I have adapted to reflect our specialized interest in practicing hospitality.[17]

1. Choose a comfortable place where you will not be interrupted for at least ten minutes for your initial prayer period. You can sit in a comfortable chair that allows you to keep your back straight and place your feet on the floor. Or you can sit on the floor in a comfortable cross-legged position. Placing a small cushion or folded blanket under your sitting bones will help you keep your spine straight. A curved back will tend to put you to sleep or will start aching; keeping your back straight but relaxed will allow good circulation of blood, oxygen, and energy throughout your body.

2. Choose the object you will focus on, whether it is a sacred word, your breath, or your inner posture of turning toward the divine presence. Whichever you choose, the purpose is to focus on your intention to become receptive to God. Through this practice you are saying yes to God, yes to the "big I," yes to the Life of life. You are making yourself available for relationality and interconnectedness.

3. Once you've selected your sacred word, take a few moments to settle into your physical posture and bring your word into your mind. You'll sit like this for ten minutes (or longer, if you want). As you sit, notice sensations in your body (for example, tired, hot, cold, stiff, thirsty) or emotions (such as feeling angry, bored, excited, sad). You may see images or notice thoughts

such as memories about the past or fantasies about the future. This is an exercise in awareness practice, as well as centering in receptivity. So when you notice that you are thinking, that your mind is drifting, that's fine. Noticing is good. Simply let go of the thoughts, and turn your attention "ever-so-gently," as Keating encourages, back to your sacred word. Turn and return to your receptive internal posture, to your sacred word, or to awareness of your breath.

No matter what you experience during these times of practice, it's okay. We do this exercise "ever-so-gently" because this is meant to be a relaxing exercise, not an opportunity to judge yourself or repress what is really happening.

4. At the end of your time, keep your eyes closed for a few extra minutes and slowly begin to bring your attention back to your surroundings. This will provide a period of transition so that the silence developed during the prayer time can be carried into the other activities of daily life.

If you continue to take the time to open yourself, the fruits of the practice will begin to show themselves in other parts of your life. You will begin to move through the world with a more grounded presence, a more relaxed posture. And if you don't notice it inside yourself, I'm guessing that the people around you will begin to notice it.

RECEPTIVITY, REVERENCE, AND GENEROSITY TO GOD IN DAILY LIFE

The more we practice receptivity, reverence, and generosity to God in times of meditation, the more we will tap into the transformative powers of spiritual hospitality. Embodying these qualities changes us, and we begin to live more centered, peaceful, joyful lives filled with the vitality of God's is-ness, the Life of life. But few of us can spend all of our time in meditation. So the question becomes, can we invite and welcome this awareness into our everyday activities and chores, such as chopping vegetables, washing dishes, and paying the bills? Yes, most definitely.

I have friends who have adopted the Hindu practice of making up a plate for God before they sit down to eat their own dinner. They give God the best portion of everything they've prepared, pour a glass of whatever they'll be drinking, even if it's just water, and set a place for God at a little altar they have in their kitchen. They call God to dinner by ringing bells, lighting candles, and waving the plate of food or a tray with lights and flowers in front of the altar. This type of action is a form of spiritual practice called *puja*, which is common in India.

They do this with great intentionality so that their actions are moving meditations, prayers in action. They're not simply going through the motions; they are turning their attention toward God with receptivity and reverence. In these ways, God is invited to be present for the sharing of food that is about to happen. When this act of invitation is finished, the food on the plate becomes God's leftovers. Since it is now God's food, mixing it back into the other food lends holiness to all the food about to be shared by the family and guests.

Although we talk about this as inviting and welcoming *God*, a practice like this changes the awareness and focus of those who are practicing it. Making this kind of gesture of invitation and welcome is an embodiment of receptivity and reverence. Extending invitation and welcome, if done with authenticity and awareness, changes *us* by changing our inner orientation toward others, the world, and the sacred that permeates life.

I often took part in a variety of practices of invitation and welcome to God when I was a resident at a meditation center for several weeks. There I immersed myself in practices of meditation, singing, and remembrance of God during chores—and discovered that this began to deepen my experience of God's presence in daily life. In the meditation center, there was a detailed schedule that shaped each day and naturally provided many opportunities for us to extend hospitality to God by inviting and welcoming God into the center of every activity of the day.

We got up early to shower, to make ourselves fresh before welcoming God to morning prayer. During chores we tried to remember God's presence, even in the most mundane of practices. God was washing the dishes with us. God was chopping the vegetables for lunch. God was cleaning the bathrooms. God was carrying wood for the fire. When it was time for a meal, we served God first. All these traditions were daily practices of remembrance of God and steadying the mind, which led to an experience similar to the one described in the biblical psalm: "I can never escape from your spirit! I can never get away from your presence!"[18]

The daily schedule in the meditation center reminded us to practice inviting and welcoming the nourishment of God's presence and the sacredness of life, even in our daily chores. You can also develop such beneficial habits by building them into the pattern of daily life at home. If you would like to try something like this, here are some ideas to get you started. But don't try too hard. Keep a light touch, and be compassionate toward yourself. Do it out of love, rather than guilt. Do it because it makes you feel good.

- Everything you do can be a prayer if you do your chores with loving attention. Begin by doing your chore a bit more slowly than you normally would. If washing the dishes, take a moment to see the dirty dishes and realize the life events that made them "dirty." Look at your hands before you use them, and realize the miracle of tendons and nerves and blood and skin and brain. Notice the blessing of running hot and cold potable water—millions of people in the world don't have this.

Touch each cup and plate you wash with awareness of every person who has touched it in the past or who may touch it in the future. See how connected we are. Ask yourself, Where is God right now?

- Take this kind of awareness out of your home and into the world by pausing for five minutes before you walk out the door. Sit in silence, turning your attention to the mysterious nature of creation. Think through the anticipated events of your day, the people you will encounter, the places you will go, and ask yourself, What would it feel like if God's love were present there? Remember these feelings as you go through your day.

- Take an extended few minutes of silence before every meal to notice your food and to notice your environment and the people you are eating with. Thich Nhat Hanh recommends breathing intentionally and smiling at every person you are eating with.[19] You don't need to rush through eating. The table is a wonderful place to take time to extend hospitality to God.

- During your dinner preparation time, turn off the radio or TV and direct your thoughts intentionally to the food you are preparing. Imagine pouring your love into the food you are washing, chopping, cooking. Even if you are opening something prepackaged, take a moment to make it more beautiful by placing it on a nice plate or in an attractive bowl. Remember that it will help fill you with *life*.

- Take ten to twenty minutes every day when you sit silently to practice holding an internal posture of receptivity and reverence toward God. For example, you can do this by practicing Centering Prayer or some other form of meditation.

- If every day is too much, commit to Centering Prayer or meditation one evening every week. Get a friend to do it with you. You can join a Centering Prayer group or meditation group so that you can get support in maintaining your practice.

- Another form of prayer you could try involves releasing the thoughts and feelings that keep you too full to perceive God or receive God's love. I do this by placing my forehead on the floor and imagining that I am pouring out all my feelings, all my experiences, and all my worries, like emptying a bucket at the feet of God. Then I rest in this emptiness, this openness, trusting that God loves me, God accepts me. Through this practice, I embody my intention to be receptive to God's presence and power. I create space—internal spaciousness—and time by simply waiting and not "doing." This is my invitation to the holy, the sacred, to enter into my awareness.

In addition to thinking about when to bring new practices and awareness into your daily life, you might also put some thought into where you pray or meditate. Here are a few suggestions.

- Your sacred space might be in the bathtub, where you nurture your body, quiet your mind, and open your heart to God.
- You can create a special prayer corner in a spare room, a place you keep clean and fill with beautiful objects, textures, or scents, to draw you into a quiet receptivity and reverence.
- A comfortable chair can be enough. Let there be one chair that you sit in for your hospitality-to-God time.
- Place a yoga mat or blanket down on the floor when it is time to pray. It's enough.
- You can look for the signs of God who is Life while walking to the bus, to the mailbox, or even while walking the dog. Consider taking a ten-minute walk at

noontime. Or take a walk with family members and when you get back home share with each other what you remember noticing. This can help you practice being aware while walking. It can also help you share your spiritual practice with your loved ones.

- An art space or craft room (or craft box stored in a closet or under the bed) can become your sacred space. I know a woman who intentionally doodles with colorful markers while she prays, expressing her hopes and dreams and gratitude in color. She welcomes God into her day through creativity.

- Your kitchen table when put to use for holy purposes is holy. Where you meditate or pray doesn't have to be separate from your life.

FINDING YOUR INNER SANCTUARY

When thinking about where to pray, another option is to create a place *inside* yourself to pray. Then, no matter where you are, you can enter into sacred space to experience the generous hospitality of God and be strengthened and healed by it. Many temples have within them an inner sanctuary that is the most sacred place in the temple. It is treated with special reverence and set aside as a place to encounter God because God is thought to live or visit there.[20] Your own heart can be such a holy place where only you can go. No human being can follow you there. It is your rendezvous point with the God who is your Source, who fills you with the Life of life. Although it is a place of solitude, your inner sanctuary is not a lonely place, but a safe place and a place of replenishment. Finding or creating such an inner space is one way to extend a generous welcome to God, which in turn will allow you to experience God's deep hospitality toward you.

To do this, get yourself situated in a quiet place where you won't be disturbed for a while. You can be seated comfortably on the floor or in a cozy chair—whatever will support you to enter your imagination.

- Begin by remembering a time when you felt at peace. For some people this might bring to mind a place in nature; for others, it might be a sleepy Saturday morning waking up to sunshine instead of an alarm clock. Take a few moments to remember the sensations in your body at that time. Allow time to remember into this experience. Think about how your shoulders felt, how your heart area felt, how your breath moved in and out of your body. Maybe the place in this memory will become your inner sanctuary. Or you can bring your feelings from this memory into another inner space.

- Carrying with you your awareness of the sensation of peacefulness and safety, search your imagination for a place that reflects that inner experience. If you don't have a memory of this feeling, now begin to imagine the kind of setting in which you could feel peaceful and safe. What colors are there? What is the light like? Are you sitting on grass or a carpet or an overstuffed chair? You may find yourself in a stone temple or in a child's tree house. You might be sitting at the side of a brook, on top of a mountain, or in a deep cave. Maybe it's a special place inside your actual house, or maybe it's in your imaginary dream house. Take some time to see, smell, hear, and feel the environment in your inner sanctuary.

- You can invite and bring people metaphorically into your inner holy space who can help you experience your intrinsic preciousness. I sometimes bow to my meditation teacher (a traditional form of greeting and sign of receptivity) when I am in my visualized inner space. I also sometimes imagine Jesus there with me. I recently read a story recounted by Jesuit priest Anthony de Mello about a man who prayed to Jesus by imagining him sitting on a nearby chair. When the man died peacefully in his bed, his daughter, who found him, said that he had pulled the nearby chair over to his bed and had lain his head out of the bed and on the chair.[21] What a comfort it must have been for him to die with his head in the lap of Jesus. Who is it that can help you realize and remember how deeply loved you are? If there is someone like that in your life, you can invite him or her to sit with you in your inner sanctuary.

Such a sanctuary may already exist for you in the physical world, so maybe it's just a matter of remembering it. For example, I once prayed in the Church of the Holy Sepulchre in Jerusalem, in the tiny room that has been built around the tomb of Jesus. Millions of people have poured out their love of God in this place. The room vibrates with those prayers. When I went in there, I was flooded with images and emotions of love and the presence of Christ. If there is a physical place like this for you, perhaps your inner sanctuary could be created by a recollection of that place. You can recreate it inside you by applying your attention to it, remembering and imagining it in great detail.

Your inner sanctuary is a safe place where you are precious, beloved, and forgiven. When you close your eyes you can go there and remember that you are good. After practicing this for a while, you'll be able to remember it even when your eyes are open.

WELCOMING GOD IN COMMUNITY THROUGH SABBATH KEEPING

In the inner sanctuary of our own hearts we can experience the generous hospitality of God and be strengthened and healed by it. Another way in which we can invite and welcome God is through the less solitary and more communal practice of keeping

Sabbath. By taking Sabbath seriously we can create space in time—an idea expressed powerfully in Abraham Joshua Heschel's classic book, *The Sabbath*. Heschel beautifully described time as "eternity in disguise"[22] and as a palace into which we step on the Sabbath to encounter the likeness of God. By keeping a Sabbath, we express our receptivity and reverence to the holy beyond the busyness of life.

Practicing Sabbath in community also gives us a way to extend the generosity of God to others—giving the gifts that we have received. When I was in graduate school, I lived with a Jewish couple who did a much better job of keeping Sabbath than I ever had before meeting them. Each Friday night we gathered around the table and lit the Sabbath candles. We welcomed this break from ordinary time, setting aside time and space to welcome the presence of God and to give thanks for God's generosity in providing bread and wine for us to share. We sat at table with guests, sharing food, conversation, and community connection.

Several things were at play in these powerful Sabbath moments. Keeping these things in mind may help you bring these practices into your own life, whether through keeping Sabbath in particular or through bringing these elements into your life through other practices.

First, we set aside time specifically for spiritual practice and awareness. In the case of keeping the Jewish Sabbath, that time was predetermined—Friday night. But for other practices, you can set your own times and patterns.

Second, we each participated through personal contemplations and prayers. When doing spiritual practices you can always make it more powerful for yourself by engaging personally and authentically. Where you place your attention will affect your experience.

And third, we did this practice together in community with friends and family. It can be very helpful to seek people with whom you can regularly practice keeping Sabbath and making room for God in your life. If you live with others, invite them to set aside regular times for sharing meals and remembering the gifts of God. This can become a family tradition if it's not already one in your family. It is also something you can do with room-mates. On the other hand, don't give this up if you live alone. Invite friends or acquaintances into patterns of community life. For example, plan to have a shared dinner once a week or once a month. Make a firm commitment to each other and support each other to spend that time well.

These practices of Sabbath keeping are strengthened when we do them together. We expect it of each other and welcome each other into the experience. In community we can set aside time to stop working, stop striving, stop achieving, and simply turn our attention toward one another and toward the sacred. In that context, our gifts to each other of food, time, and attention are an extension of God's gifts to us, a reflection of the Life of life. In and through our community experience, we are gathered and bound together, to use the language of Hildegard of Bingen, into the Life of God that nurtures every living creature. Community Sabbath keeping is another way to practice recep-tivity, reverence, and generosity to the holy, and through it, we are shaped as people of deep hospitality.

CHAPTER TWO

HOSPITALITY TO SELF

Inviting the Authentic Self

O pportunities for hospitality sneak up on us all the time, and they always offer us a choice about how we will respond. Sometimes these opportunities are very close to home and begin with extending hospitality to ourselves. Hospitality to the self has the basic movement of in-with-out, even though it may seem paradoxical to suggest reaching *out* to the *inner* self. Nevertheless, the receptivity, reverence, and generosity that we show to ourselves will act as a sure foundation for the hospitality that we extend to those in the ever-widening circles of relationship in our lives. Hospitality begins in our spiritual core, where we discover a true self that is deeply connected with divinity. Offering receptivity, reverence, and generosity to the self helps us to love and accept ourselves, to heal and discover a deeper, broader, bigger self than we knew we were. This true self, deeply connected with God and love, becomes the great source of hospitality within us. A story from my own life may help demonstrate what I mean.

When my faith community was very young, we decided to gather for meals and conversation two Sunday evenings a month. It was a good idea, but it was also a new idea that we had no experience with, and we hadn't thought through *how* we were going to pull these meals together. Who would host? Who would cook? We were a small group, and so, wanting to be hospitable, I stepped into the gap and offered to cook the first meal ... and the second meal ... and the third, and on and on for several long months. As I grew more and more depleted I realized that this wasn't hospitable at all! Rather than giving from a deep, full source that was within me, yet greater than me, I was operating under my own power, simply giving myself away, bit by bit. In an attempt to be generous to others I was not being receptive, reverent, *or* generous to myself, and this began to turn my attempted hospitality into more of a punishment of myself as I continued doing it. In a situation like that, what would hospitality to the self look like?

I began to find out one summer afternoon when I felt I just couldn't go on like that anymore. Once again, I was responsible for preparing a meal for that very evening, but I was exhausted and drained and even starting to feel resentful that no one was helping me. I felt very lonely preparing the meals like this. What was intended to be connective and life-giving had become for me isolating and a burden. Instead of pushing this out of my consciousness when I felt it gnawing at the edges of my mind, as I had been for weeks, I stopped rushing around and just sat down to think about—become aware of—what was happening and how I felt.

This is the essence of receptivity and the first step of hospitality: *awareness of what is*—without judgment, repression, or denial. Instead of focusing on other people and trying to blame them for not chipping in and helping out, I kept the focus on myself and examined the tangle of emotions I was having. I've mentioned several already: resentment, exhaustion, a sense of being drained. I also became aware that I had created the

circumstances by not asking for help. I recognized my own cul-
pability and my own power in getting myself into this situation.
When we allow ourselves to become aware like this, we become
receptive to reality as it is, not as we want it to be. We are able to
perceive a situation, ourselves, and others with greater fullness
and accuracy.

Developing this kind of *receptivity* enables us to see the situation clearly without judgment. In turn, this allows us to move on
to the second stage of hospitality—*reverence*. When I acknowledged my own role in creating the situation, I became able to take
a step that denial would have prevented. I became able to forgive
myself. Reverence is an action of the heart that often manifests as
compassionate acceptance—and acceptance is key in this second
stage of hospitality. Rather than rejecting myself, criticizing and
emotionally beating myself up, I accepted myself, flaws and all.
This allowed me to be truly *with* myself, the real me—not the me
I wished I was or pretended to be, but the real me, imperfect as I
am. Faced with cooking yet one more dinner, I decided to love
myself in spite of my failures, fatigue, and resentment. This
allowed me to move into the third stage of hospitality—*generosity*.

Generosity is present or not based on how we choose to act.
I could have run out to the supermarket to buy canned soup and
a bag of salad greens, something quick and easy, but instead I
decided to be generous to myself by nurturing myself all the way
through the dinner preparations. Since I was going to be cooking anyway, I thought, what if I applied my intention to making
the food physically beautiful and delicious? What if, instead of
harboring resentment while cooking, I poured my love for the
community into the food? What if I focused on making the most
beautiful, nourishing food I could pull off?

This changed my entire day. I had a party with myself,
preparing a celebratory feast. I shopped for organic fresh foods;
made a loaf of fresh bread (in the bread machine); created a
vibrant green salad with crispy romaine lettuce, organic pear

slices, fresh (not dried) fig chunks, and homemade sweet balsamic vinaigrette dressing; and finally, made a cool tomato summer soup with fresh corn thrown in at the last minute so that it maintained its summery sweetness.

When I was done cooking, I had been nurtured by the beautiful colors and textures of the food. I felt energized, rather than drained, and I knew that others would be nourished by the meal as well. In responding to my situation like this, with receptivity, reverence, and generosity, I was offering hospitality to myself by creating a warm and nurturing environment in which to dwell and be renewed.

Receptivity: An Invitation to the Authentic Self

In general, becoming receptive is preparing ourselves to invite others into our lives and hearts. It is taking an invitational inner posture. In terms of receptivity to the self, it means recognizing and acknowledging what is really going on inside of us. This is how we hold a posture of invitation toward the authentic self. Sometimes, however, it takes someone else seeing us deeply before we can really see ourselves. I had an experience like this once with my meditation teacher early in our relationship. I was visiting her retreat center, along with about two thousand other people. Many people from around the world were seeking a few moments with her, attending classes taught by the monks of her lineage and public talks that she herself offered. After one of these public programs, people were queued up in long lines, waiting to greet her, share some news, or ask her a question. She sat in a chair while five people at a time gathered around her. She interacted with each person individually, if only to acknowledge his or her greeting. She sat like this for as long as it took to greet and receive each person.

Being one of at least a thousand people who wanted to greet her on this particular day, I waited in line for a long time.

Although I had been deeply touched by her presence and her teachings, I had never spoken a word to her personally. On this day, I wanted to give her a card in which I had written a prayer. But I was very nervous. Classic worries ran through my mind such as, what if she doesn't like me? What if I do something wrong? It was a bit like being on a first date with someone you really like, and a thousand other people are tagging along to see how it goes.

When I finally got to the front of the line, I went toward her chair and made the customary bow, people on either side of me greeting her in the same way. I sat up on my knees and held out the card I had for her, but she was busy talking to several people on the other side of her chair. This was my social nightmare. I was mutely holding out the card toward her, she was looking the other way, and crowds of people were gathered around us, seeing it all. They were seeing me, actually. That was my fear. I felt completely exposed and vulnerable. I could wait in the crowd to get to this moment, but once I was up there, I could not wait any longer. I was in it. I was on the spot. The heat began building in my face. My body began to sweat. More than anything in the world I wanted her to turn to me, to be so happy to see me, to affirm me, smile, and take the card. But she was busy.

Ten seconds is a very long time to be on your knees holding out a card for someone who is not looking at you, while crowds of people watch. Fifteen seconds seems unbearable. So I interrupted her; I said her name, but she ignored me. Twenty seconds is an eternity. Maybe she didn't hear me, since she was chatting and laughing with the people on the other side of her chair. So I said her name again, louder this time. She ignored me. I thought I would die. I thought I might burst into flames at any moment, my embarrassment was so great. It felt like my body was on fire and my mind had stopped working. I had only one goal in life and that was to get this card into her hand and get out of there.

Against all forces of wisdom, I repeated her name a third time, at which point she stopped talking with the others and it seemed everything in the world stopped as well. I imagine that everyone in the huge hall stopped talking and an incredible hush filled the room. But more likely it was the roaring that was happening in my ears that prevented me from hearing anything. My vision narrowed too, as it does when a person is about to lose consciousness. I could only see her, as she turned toward me and looked into my eyes. I looked back without saying anything. Our eyes were locked. At one moment her eyes flitted down to the card still held out toward her with my outstretched arm, but flew instantly back up to my eyes. She didn't move and I didn't move.

She looked at me until all that existed was her *looking*. She was looking at me, and I was looking at her. We saw each other and that was all there was—looking and seeing. Some unnameable deep place in her was looking directly into some unnameable deep place in me. This was an unbreakable connection. In this deep place between and behind our eyes it was quiet and still and strong, while all around me the fire of my own humiliation raged. She did not look away, and she did not submit to my need to disappear by taking the card from my hand. She saw me, until I began to see myself. It took me years to understand this moment, but it changed me instantly, because it gave me an experience of being deeply connected, from the center of my being to the center of her being. Shame and fear and humiliation and the desperate need to be invisible in order to be safe could not break the connection to this deep core of my being. She connected to it, and this connected me to myself.

Finally, she turned to one of her assistants who instantly took the card from me. I gave the normal bow and the room became animated again. Back at my seat, I cried and cried, feeling the shame and humiliation wash over me. I saw, as though for the first time, how my actions had been completely controlled by my fear of these feelings. I would have done anything to avoid feeling them. When I was holding out the card to her I was not able to accurately perceive what was happening. I didn't notice that I was afraid and accept that feeling within myself. I didn't notice that I was perfectly fine waiting my turn like everyone else was. Neither did I notice that she was busy with other people who needed and deserved her attention as much as I did. Instead, I falsely perceived that I was in serious danger of some kind of public shame, which I then actually *created* by repeatedly interrupting her. If only I had been able to recognize my feelings and accept them rather than try to avoid them, things might have turned out differently. Trying to escape them actually gave them power over me and the situation.

In retrospect, I can look deeply into the source of those feelings of fear and shame, and I find that they are connected to a deeply internalized feeling of not being good enough, of not being lovable or likable, and of feeling ashamed of those supposed inadequacies. I was afraid of being rejected. My teacher's strong and steady gaze directly contradicted my fear of rejection, in that she stayed connected with me through the whole fiery ordeal. She didn't need to say anything to chastise me, because her looking at what was happening and *seeing* me caused me to see what I was doing. She didn't reject or even rebuke me. She simply saw what was happening. And this is what we can do for ourselves as well—simply see what is happening and not run away. We don't have to reject and rebuke ourselves. Instead, we can be present, aware, receptive. This is how we can invite our authentic selves to come out of hiding. This invitation is the first step of hospitality to the self.

ENGAGING THE SHADOW PLACES

As my story shows, it's not always easy to be receptive to and accepting of our authentic, whole selves, because our whole selves include things that are painful to see. I had to pass through the fires of humiliation to learn how to recognize my feelings before I could begin to let them go and live from a different, deeper, and more whole place. Benedictine monk Daniel Homan and Lonni Collins Pratt, in their book *Radical Hospitality*, remind us that "there is a kind of gentle hospitality with the self that most of us fail to practice. You know that moment you look in the mirror and see a stranger staring out those eyes? We don't accept the stranger within. We dread the regions of ourselves we don't understand."[1] Those regions we dread are the shadowy places in us, where fear lives, anger rages, and shame drags us down. It is easier to look the other way and not shine the light of our awareness into these unpleasant feelings. But the shadows don't go away until a light shines into them.

When I interrupted my meditation teacher repeatedly to try to avoid being visible and vulnerable, I was being controlled by my humiliation and my fear of being judged and rejected. Although my interaction with her gave me new insight into myself, these limiting feelings of fear and shame did not disappear from my life forever at that moment. I had to keep working with them in order to become more aware of and more free from them. Emotions and thoughts that undermine our receptivity, reverence, and generosity will continue to come up in us all of our lives. Developing skills for dealing with them will enable us to more fully embody hospitality to the self.

THICH NHAT HANH'S FIVE STEPS FOR TRANSFORMING FEELINGS

Thich Nhat Hanh, a Vietnamese Buddhist monk, has described a method for engaging some of the thoughts and emotions that can pull us away from our true self. He talks about transforming our feelings as a way of learning to be at peace within ourselves.[2] His suggested process is very relevant to our study of hospitality in that these steps are a practical way to engage the shadow places inside ourselves and pass through them into the realm of hospitality.

Here is a synopsis of his suggested five-step practice. You can begin to practice these steps any time you notice yourself having a particularly strong emotion.

1. **Recognize the feeling.** Notice and name what you are feeling. Both the act of noticing, which Nhat Hanh calls *mindfulness*, as well as the *feeling* you are noticing (for example, fear), coexist within you. Simply recognize them both inside you, as though you were saying to yourself: I *notice* that I am *feeling* afraid.

2. **Become one with the feeling.** He describes this as greeting your emotion, "Hello, Fear. How are you today?" rather than telling it, "Go away ... I don't like you. You are not me." Instead, accept your feeling as though it *is* you. Accepting what is within us is a way that we accept ourselves, as imperfect and messy as we are. "If we try to throw away what we don't want" within ourselves, Thich Nhat Hanh says, "we may throw away most of ourselves."[3] This kind of self-rejection is the opposite of hospitality. Instead, simply attend to your feeling. Greet it, and accept it.

3. **Calm the feeling.** Just by giving your attention to the feeling, it begins to calm down. Also, it will help to focus on your breath. When you breathe in, imagine your breath flowing to all parts of your body, calming you. When you breathe out, let your fear dissipate the way your breath dissipates into the atmosphere. When you notice your fear (or anger, or whatever), awareness and fear meet inside you, and fear begins to control you less and less. Fear, when it is greeted and witnessed in this way, becomes less afraid; anger becomes less angry.

4. **Release the feeling.** Let it go. Paradoxically, by allowing the feeling to be in you without pushing it away, it seems to fade away on its own. This may be counterintuitive, but the harder we try to push feelings away, the more they stick with us. Pushing away is a form of clinging, a way that we stay engaged with, focused on, and attached to a feeling. By accepting feelings and noticing them, it is easier to let go of them.

5. **Look deeply to see the source of the feeling.** This is the step that can really change us. While calming and releasing are good ways to deal with feelings when they come up, they don't address the causes or sources of our feelings. So when you are feeling fearful, ask yourself what you are afraid of and why you are afraid of it. When you notice that you are feeling angry, you may think it is obvious what you are angry about. But why does that thing make you angry? What are the thoughts and feelings associated with that anger? Looking deeply into the causes of our feelings often reveals that our feelings are based on inaccurate perceptions or suppressed memories of things that are no longer true. When we realize this, our feelings begin to have less power to control us in the way that my unacknowledged fears controlled me in the incident with my meditation teacher.

Becoming aware of our thoughts and feelings is equivalent to extending an invitation to our authentic self. Taking this kind of receptive posture is the beginning of hospitality to the self.

REVERENCE: WELCOMING THE SELF IN SPIRITUAL SOLITUDE

Hospitality to the self includes all the elements of receptivity, reverence, and generosity. Once we have invited the self to show up more fully through our practices of receptive awareness, the second step of hospitality is to welcome the self in reverence. Truly welcoming the self will become the foundation of our capacity to welcome others as we begin to extend hospitality into the ever-expanding circles of relationships in our lives.

Catholic priest and theologian Henri Nouwen refers to an inner sacred experience he calls *receptive solitude*, a state of being that grows in us as we become centered in inner quiet.[4] To engage our own solitude, we must take the time to become still, to recognize and accept our human nature, limitations and all. It involves receptivity because we first become aware of our human nature. But the spiritual solitude Nouwen describes moves beyond mere receptive awareness into the realm of reverence, the realm of compassionate acceptance and love. Solitude is not a lonely place, because when we find it, we come to feel our deep interconnectedness with all people and all things. In solitude we are not depleted because we tap into a source of vitality and love that is larger than our individual self. Welcoming the self in inner solitude will paradoxically lead to being more connected to others and to life itself.

Nouwen calls the opposite of receptive solitude a "suffocating loneliness," which affects more of us than we would like to admit. I have an old friend named Susan who recently described her confusion at finding herself unhappy in a fifteen-year relationship that she says "looks beautiful" on the outside. "I have everything I could ever want," she told me. And yet, as we allowed time and space to reflect on her experience, she went on to say that she didn't know what she was longing for. Apparently, she didn't have everything that she could want. She wanted herself, she said, but thought that would be selfish. Instead, she had somehow given herself away. Even in the context of a "good" relationship, Susan was feeling a quietly desperate loneliness.

Like many women—and men, for that matter—she had taught herself so thoroughly how to act happy and "be nice" that she was no longer sure what she truly felt. This is the equivalent of shutting the door in the face of your own self. By not accepting and welcoming the authentic self with reverence and love, our experience of that self begins to diminish and a kind of empty feeling takes its place, a suffocating loneliness.

External things can never really fill that inner void we feel. As long as we do not invite and welcome our true self to show up, other relationships won't fill the emptiness either. Nouwen describes the suffocating loneliness like this: "No friend or lover, no husband or wife, no community or commune will be able to put to rest our deepest cravings for unity and wholeness. And by burdening others with these divine expectations, of which we ourselves are often only partially aware, we might inhibit the expression of free friendship and love and evoke instead feelings of inadequacy and weakness. Friendship and love cannot develop in the form of an anxious clinging to each other. They ask for gentle fearless space in which we can move to and from each other."[5]

Dwelling in spiritual solitude—or receptive solitude, as Nouwen calls it—can also be described as dwelling in this gentle fearless space. This is the space of true hospitality. When we dwell in the solitude of the soul, we tap into a deep resource and become free of debilitating neediness. In this gentle fearless space we realize our intrinsic goodness and embrace our identity as unconditionally lovable and deeply interconnected with God, the Life of life, and the whole of creation. When Nouwen describes our "deepest cravings for unity and wholeness" as "divine expectations," he is reminding us that our relationship with the Divine is the place where our deepest cravings for unity and wholeness are met. The communion we seek is not possible when limited to another human being or any external thing. Our wholeness is based on the identity of the true self. "Who am I?" Nouwen asks on behalf of us all. "I am the beloved," the deepest self answers.[6] Knowing this sets us free to succeed or fail without ever losing that identity, because our identity is not dependent on success or failure or any external thing.

While Nouwen encourages us to claim that identity, theologian Paul Tillich describes this state of belovedness as a gift of grace: "[I]t is as though a voice were saying: 'You are accepted, accepted by that which is greater than you, and the name of which you do not know. Do not ask for the name now; perhaps you will find it later.'" If we can simply accept the fact that we are accepted, Tillich says, then we will experience grace.[7] This love relationship with God in which we are accepted is a preexisting relationship. It's something that always was and always is, as we began to see in chapter 1. There's nothing we can do to make it go away, and there's nothing we need to do to make it true. It is the nature of the self to inter-exist with God in love. The question is, will we accept the acceptance; will we listen to the voice of the One calling us beloved?

THE SALT DOLL FINDS HER TRUE SELF

Once a salt doll approached the ocean with awe. "What are you?" the doll asked the ocean, overwhelmed by its sheer magnitude. Something about the ocean fascinated her; she felt an affinity with it, felt drawn to it. The ocean didn't try to explain but simply invited the doll into itself to find out for herself what it was.

As the doll walked into the water, she found that she began to dissolve. Her feet and her hands became smaller. Her hair began to disappear. She felt a strange mix of fear and longing as the ocean began to enter her body and she began to know, to catch a glimpse of her true self in the ocean. She was made of what the ocean was made of, salt. But the ocean was more than salt. It was also water. It was also minerals and plants and other creatures. The ocean was filled with life. As the body of the salt doll dissolved, she didn't disappear. She felt her consciousness expanding and permeating the ocean. The salt doll let go of her small self, her small identity, and allowed herself to became part of something greater. She became the vast ocean, filled with an abundance of life.

The Greek Fathers of the Eastern Orthodox Church have made a theological distinction between the *image* of God, which is how we are created, and the *likeness* of God, which is what we would become if we fully actualized the image given to us at our creation. The *image* contains the potential of God, and the *likeness* is its realization, its full manifestation.[8] The salt doll, being made of the same salt that filled the ocean, was in some ways made in the image of the ocean. She was less than the ocean, and clearly she didn't have all the qualities of the ocean. But when she entered the ocean and the ocean entered her, she became the full likeness of the ocean.

Hindu scriptures called the Upanishads also try to evoke this relationship between the small, individual self, and the great, true self, the fullness of existence. The Upanishads say, "The little space within the heart is as great as this vast universe. The heavens and the earth are there, and the sun, and the moon, and the stars; fire and lightning and winds are there; and all that now is and all that is now: for the whole universe is in him, [the one who] dwells within our heart."[9] Finding the universe within ourselves may sound like a tall order, but it flows naturally from the very act of looking within and trusting what we find there.

My friend Susan's story is very different from the salt doll's story. Susan was wondering who she was after fifteen years in a "perfect" relationship. She had lost her sense of self, not through greater awareness, but by suppressing awareness of her feelings and greatest longings. Susan stayed in her relationship, giving and giving without tapping into the deeper source of love and wholeness that is inside herself, much as I continued cooking meals without calling on the source of generosity that was inside me. That would be like the salt doll staying small, never entering the ocean and finding out who she truly was.

The story of the salt doll is not about losing yourself in the sense of giving and giving until you disappear. It's about becoming bigger than you think you are; it's about welcoming God and welcoming self to come together inside us. Thomas Merton said that self-realization is "less an awareness of ourselves than it is an awareness of the God to whom we are drawn in the depths of our own being. We become real, and experience our actuality, not when we pause to reflect upon our own self as an isolated individual entity, but rather when, transcending ourselves and passing beyond reflection, we center our whole soul upon the God who is our life."[10]

The more we are able to share in this divine life, to grow into the likeness of God, the more we discover who we are. We discover our own center, intermingled in some mysterious way with the center of God. This receptive solitude is where we receive the love that has our name on it. In this solitude, we grow to accept that we are accepted. Merton said that "the recognition of our true self, in the divine image, is then a recognition of the fact that we are known and loved by God."[11] Solitude becomes the reverent space in our hearts where we know that we ourselves are loved, accepted, and, in the deepest sense, at home. Developing this reverence and tapping into this divine acceptance is the important middle step of hospitality to the self.

ENTERING A RECEPTIVE, REVERENT SPACE THROUGH MANTRA REPETITION

But how do we draw close to that reverent space inside us? How can we, like the salt doll, begin the process of discovering our larger selves and letting go of the things that keep us small and isolated? One practice that can help is simple prayer or mantra repetition. This is a basic technique for stilling and focusing the mind as well as shifting perspective to create a new space inside yourself in which to welcome your deep true self. In chapter 1, we learned about holding a sacred word in mind for the practice of Centering Prayer. A mantra can be as simple as such a word, or it can be a phrase in any language. It gives your mind something to hold on to when emotions wash over you. When you repeat a mantra very often, it becomes part of you and begins to come to your aid when you are feeling impatient, overwhelmed, angry, or afraid (to name just a few possibilities).

Many kinds of prayer that involve repetition and the counting of beads play this sort of role in spiritual life. Repetitions begin to take on a power of their own, changing the person repeating them, stilling and redirecting the mind and heart. Through repetition we can let the truth of the words we are saying descend from our mind into our heart. In this way, our words stop being simply words and become transformative prayers, fostering awareness (receptivity) and compassionate acceptance (reverence) of whatever we encounter.

Try the following exercise and see how it affects you over time. The more you repeat a particular prayer or mantra, the more it will take up residence in you, and the more powerful and transformative it will become in your life. After a while, if this technique works for you, you will begin to return to your prayer or mantra without even trying. The first time you try this, select a time and place where you can practice for ten minutes in an uninterrupted and focused way.

1. Choose a simple prayer or mantra on which you will focus. Settle on one that you will use for your first try and commit to it for this whole exercise. You want to allow the meanings of the words to settle into your heart so that you can discover the truth in them. If the prayer you try doesn't feel right, you can always select a different one for your next practice session. But keep in mind that you will have the best results by selecting a word or phrase and sticking with it—preferably for six months or more.

2. Your own mantra or simple prayer could be a complete phrase, such as "Peace in every step, peace in
   every step," or "Rest in presence." Or it could be a par-
   tial phrase that references something longer, such as
   "Only in God, only in God," reminding you that "only
   in God I find rest and peace." Select something that
   has an easy rhythm and a significant spiritual meaning
   for you. Anything can become a simple prayer that
   you turn to again and again.

3. To begin, take a comfortable seated posture. If you are
   sitting on the floor, you can sit in a simple cross-legged
   position. You might want to place a small pillow or
   blanket under your sitting bones to lift you off the
   floor a bit. This will make it easier to keep a straight
   back. If seated in a chair, place both feet on the floor.

4. Take a moment to focus on your breath. Notice your in-
   breath and your out-breath. Make a full, long exhale,
   pushing all the air out of your lungs and holding this
   emptiness for a moment or two. This creates space for
   new air, which your body will naturally take in. You
   may find that you breathe a bit more deeply after
   doing this.

5. Then begin to add your mantra or simple prayer to
   your focus on the breath, repeating silently, for example, "Only in God" on the in-breath and "Only in
   God" on the out-breath.

6. When you notice that your mind has begun wander-
   ing, great! You noticed! Don't worry about it or
   judge it—the mind is created to think. We aren't trying to stop the mind from being the mind, we're
   practicing focusing the mind and discovering the
   power inside our simple prayer. Simply return your
   attention to your breath and to your mantra.
   Continue this practice for ten minutes. As you gain

more experience with this, you may find you want to continue longer.

After practicing this a few times, begin trying it in the middle of your day. Wherever you are, you can turn to your mantra for support. When your thoughts or feelings overwhelm you, repeat your mantra or simple prayer. It stills and focuses the mind and can bring you to a new place.

Other methods of practice include chanting or singing your prayer. This will open you up if you can surrender to the process. Allow the air to pass over your lips. Let sound and vibration resonate through your body. Let go of your inhibitions about being heard. This is about expression and transformation. *Nama sankirtana*, a Hindu practice of chanting the names of God, has been quite transformative in my life. In the Christian tradition, there is a community of ecumenical monks in Taizé, France, who have developed a style of praying through short repetitive chants that function in a similar way—allowing us to relax into and internalize the deeper meanings of the prayers. An example of a line from a Taizé chant is: "In God alone my soul can find rest and peace."[12]

Through these practices we extend hospitality to ourselves by fostering reverence and helping ourselves remember the abundant life and generous love that surround us and hold us. If we only repeat any of these prayers a few times, it's quite likely that they will remain intellectual, up in our heads. Then they might function more like resolutions that we have trouble keeping, or affirmations that we have trouble believing. In contrast, Henri Nouwen used "The Lord is my shepherd" as his mantra for two years.[13] In describing this kind of prayer, he said, "If we keep saying the truth, the real truth—'The Lord is my shepherd; there is nothing I shall want'—and let that truth descend from our mind into our heart, gradually those words are written on the walls of our inner holy place. That becomes the space in which we can receive our colleagues and our work, our family and our friends, and the people whom we will meet during the day."[14] That becomes our place of receptivity and reverence, our inner holy place, the place of sacred solitude in which we can truly welcome our self and offer generous nurture.

GENEROSITY: NURTURING THE SELF

Generosity is the completion of the cycle of hospitality. It is made up of our actions toward those whom we are welcoming—an outflow of physical, spiritual, and emotional care and nurture. Generosity involves giving a little bit more than we think we can, but in hospitality to the self this doesn't mean giving it away. This is the paradox of offering "out" to the inner self—generosity in this case means deeply taking in the nurturance that will make us whole. This is how we offer the generosity of hospitality to the self.

While this nurturance often comes through specifically spiritual practices such as prayer or mantra repetition, meditation or chanting and singing, it also comes through very physical, practical practices. Generosity is based on the outward actions we take toward ourselves and others. Being generous toward ourselves in a physical way—by honoring our bodies and taking care of them—is a wonderful way to bring the practice of hospitality to ourselves full circle and revere the holy in us. To expand this practice in your own life, consider focusing on the following areas:

Be devoted to feeding yourself. Eating can be a form of art and play, devotion and commitment to yourself. It can nourish you on the physical, emotional, and spiritual levels all at once. Try to get in touch with the nourishing role that food can play in your life by cooking for yourself, letting others cook for you, or sharing a meal with loved ones. Make it special by paying attention to how the food looks. Don't just eat it out of the cardboard take-out box or the sauce pan you cooked it in. Consciously direct your love into the preparation and presentation of your food, knowing that this love-food will also nourish your body. Love your body by loving your food. Here's a time when it is okay to play with your food!

Honor your body by letting it rest. Allow yourself to sleep without an alarm clock at least once a week. Try to be disciplined about going to bed early enough to feel rested when you wake up. Whether you need six, eight, or ten hours of sleep to be at your best, figure out a way to pattern your life so that you can get these precious and healing hours of sleep.

Honor your body by letting it *move*. Our bodies are complex organisms with muscles made for all kinds of movement. Walk, dance, run, work out, play sports, hike, bike—but don't make this a second job. Let these activities be forms of play and sources of enjoyment and refreshment in your life.

Welcome your true feelings, even the unpleasant ones. Write them down. Take a personal inventory. Acknowledge your power, the role you play in creating the situations you face in your life. If you have made mistakes, accept that as fundamentally human, let yourself grow in awareness, and prepare to make better decisions in the future. Accept yourself; forgive yourself.

Make a list of feeling words and consult it when needed. If you have difficulty identifying your feelings, perhaps your emotional vocabulary can be expanded. Try making a list of every feeling word you can think of. Consult a thesaurus if you get stuck. Watch for feeling words in things you are reading. Try to fill a page with multiple columns of words. Then, when you don't know what you're feeling, you can "check the list." Make it a game, joke around with friends and loved ones about it, but check the list when you need to. Here are a few words to get you started: *happy, sad, angry, confused, irritated, nervous, afraid, anxious, infuriated, frustrated, ecstatic, overjoyed, excited, curious, lost, lonely, depressed, grieving, overwhelmed, content, peaceful.* Developing the capacity to identify your feelings will help you grow in self-awareness, move toward self-acceptance, and ultimately love yourself and others with generosity.

Express love and affection toward yourself. Do this as you might toward a lover. Write a letter to yourself, saying what you long to hear. Write a letter to someone you love, sharing some part of yourself that you long to be known. Or better yet, have dinner together and tell this special person what is in your heart and on your mind. Practice physically nurturing yourself with tea, baths, cuddly blankets, naps, colors, scents, or delicious foods. Make a list of things you admire about yourself. These are all ways of being receptive to your inner being, holding yourself in reverence, and generously giving to yourself.

Make dates with yourself. Write yourself into your calendar and commit to spending time alone staring off into space and doing nothing. Or plan something fun. Put as much thought into it as you would if you were going on a date with a loved one. After all, aren't *you* a loved one of yourself? How about a concert? A day at the museum? A picnic at the beach? Go. Do.

Take some time alone in your inner sanctuary. Whether you do this by sitting in meditation or taking yourself on a brisk walk, setting aside time to pray and open yourself to the God who loves you is a form of spiritual nurture. Be generous in giving this to yourself. Remember the Life of life in whom you live and move and have your being. You are a precious part of the whole of Life.

THE HEART IS THE HUB OF ALL SACRED PLACES

A wonderful inscription over the door to a temple that I have often visited says, "The heart is the hub of all sacred places. Go there and roam."[15] Hospitality to the self is deeply interconnected with hospitality to God, because deep within our heart—the core of our being—God dwells. Reaching deep within we find our greatest source of hospitality. It is the potential of God, the power and life and love of God, with which we are deeply connected. Being open and receptive to that reality, holding the mysterious presence of inner sacredness with reverence, and allowing it to nurture us generously will begin to form us into its own shape.

CHAPTER THREE

HOSPITALITY TO FAMILY

Offering Full Presence to Those Closest to Us

Hospitality to the self leads naturally into hospitality to the family. While spiritual solitude is the space in our own hearts where we come to know ourselves as beloved and at home in the deepest sense, it is in our physical homes that we begin to encounter other hearts—other people—with whom we are deeply connected. Our families are made up of the relationships in which we are generally the most deeply known, and which fill large spans of our lives. For our purposes here, consider your family to be the people that you live with or have lived with, those to whom you are connected or committed by choice or by birth. Maybe you are married and living with children, married without children, living in a domestic partnership, or living in your parents' home or with your parents or other extended family members in your own home. Or maybe you are single and living alone or living with a good friend—the details are less important than the quality of your relationships. Where is there a shared intimacy? That is where your family is.

All of our families look different. Your family (in the general sense) may include a large extended family. In my case, I have eighty-three first cousins, most of whom have spouses and several children, some of whom I have never met. To be honest, I could pass some of my relatives on the street and not recognize them. But this is not the part of family that I am addressing here. This chapter is about hospitality in intimate and close relationships; for me, family means my parents, sisters and brothers, nieces and nephews, and some friends and their children with whom I have lived in the past. For you it probably means something else.

THE VULNERABILITY OF BEING KNOWN

Family is one place where our messiness is most visible, and I don't just mean papers strewn about the house. I mean messiness in our emotional lives. Everything isn't neat and tidy here; our foibles come to the fore. These relationships are so vitally important in our lives precisely because in them our real humanness—vulnerability and fallibility included—is seen and known and embraced (or not). Home can be one of the hardest places to maintain a hospitable heart—precisely because so much is at stake. Sometimes it might seem much easier to make ourselves vulnerable to a stranger than to someone we love. It seems counterintuitive on the surface, but let's look more deeply into the idea.

I once had a friend who was incredibly warm and outgoing. This was what drew me to her in the first place. She was like a beacon of light. Everyone wanted to talk with her, because her graciousness made them feel warm and happy. They felt honored and likable. As I became better friends with her, though, I began to see the cracks in the foundation of her generosity. She began to share stories with me of her upbringing, ways she had been mistreated, fears that had been instilled in her. She confessed that she was able to be relaxed and gracious with children and strangers because they could not "hurt" her—they had no emotional power over her and couldn't reject her. They didn't make her feel vulnerable and afraid.

When she began to feel that someone truly cared for her, and when she began to care more deeply for another person, she began to expect the brokenness of her childhood to repeat itself. She suspected that the person she cared for was not reliable, and that if she truly became vulnerable, she would be deeply wounded yet again. It wasn't easy for her to remain authentically present and self-aware in these deepening relationships, and fear, anger, and shame began to replace trust, honesty, and joy at the center of her interactions. Because of this pattern of action on her part, she had also developed a history of relationships falling apart exactly when you would expect them to be growing stronger.

Her story presents a good example of the difference between genuine hospitality and the mere appearance of it. With people who don't know us well, we can appear to be very "hospitable," going through the motions of hospitality by throwing dinner parties, facilitating great conversations, and making ourselves seem more confident, kind, and generous than we really feel inside. But when we are alone with our families, our deeper frailties can begin to show. Openness, trust, and honesty might get squeezed out by fear, anger, or shame. We may suddenly get "too busy" to be fully present with those we love. We may be concerned that if we show our deepest weaknesses we won't be able to fulfill our family responsibilities, or that we may be judged by those whose love we need so very much. We may become emotionally distant in order to hide our weaknesses or self-doubts. These seemingly self-protective measures inevitably end up isolating and weakening us, rather than strengthening us in our foundation or core self. All of them indicate that we are not practicing receptivity, reverence, and generosity toward the self or God, and that prevents us from offering real hospitality to our families. But this is something that we can change.

In earlier chapters we've touched on practices that develop awareness, compassionate acceptance, and conscious acts of nurturing as alternatives to the sometimes unhealthy and unconscious ways we deal with life. In this chapter, we'll consider an easy way to remember the steps for practicing hospitality—the three A's—*awareness, acceptance, action.* Now that we're exploring relationships with others, you may find yourself falling into emotionally intense situations when you need something simple to hang on to. When you find yourself in the midst of fear, anger, frustration, or similar emotions, just remember the three A's and return to the present moment, here and now. Begin with awareness and notice. From the place of awareness you can learn to uncover compassionate acceptance and make thoughtful choices about the actions you will take.[1] This is a foundational practice for developing receptivity, reverence, and generosity and will come up again and again as we continue to explore hospitality in the ever-larger circles of relationship in our lives.

APPLY AWARENESS TO DEVELOP RECEPTIVITY

Receptivity is based in a full awareness that allows us to perceive ourselves, a situation, and each other accurately. This is the "in" part of in-with-out. It is essential in developing an invitational inner posture because a sincere invitation is based in authenticity and honesty, both of which are based on self-awareness. In other words, if you're not insightfully aware of your thoughts, assumptions, and feelings, you might unconsciously act them out the way I "acted out" my fears by interrupting my meditation teacher in the story in chapter 2. When we are able to witness and name our thoughts and feelings, we realize that we don't have to express them all or be controlled by them. When we become aware of what is happening inside us and what is happening between ourself and another person, then we become available in the present moment in a real way. Simple awareness practice is a foundational building block in the spiritual practice of hospitality because it begins to teach you how to be awake and aware in the present moment. This is an essential skill that will enable you to be fully present with your family members in the here and now. Without the ability to be awake and aware in the present moment, you might get so busy with your memories, fantasies, fears, assumptions, and judgments that you forget to look into the eyes of your loved ones and really *see* them.

To practice receptivity, you can begin with simple awareness exercises. Thoughts come in a variety of types—memories, fantasies, imaginings, beliefs, judgments, assumptions, images, and stories we tell ourselves, to name just a few. Similarly, there is a wide range of feelings as we explored in chapter 2 through the creation of a list of feeling words. To practice applying simple awareness, try this simple five-minute exercise. Wherever you are—seated at your desk, riding your bike, or cooking supper—focus only on the present moment. Here are some questions to ask yourself to help you do this:

- What do you see? Notice textures, colors, shapes.
- What do you hear? Notice sounds near you and in the distance. Notice silence if there is any. Try to be simultaneously aware of what you see and what you hear. Can you do it?
- What do you smell or taste? Anything?
- What do you feel physically? If you're sitting at your desk, what does the surface of the desk feel like? If you're taking out the garbage, notice the feeling of the garbage bag in your hand; notice the sensation of the bottoms of your feet touching the ground.
- What do you feel emotionally? In this exercise we treat emotions as sensations or thoughts; notice them, name them, then return to awareness of what you perceive here, right now.

As you proceed with this exercise you may become suddenly aware that you are no longer noticing what you see and hear. Instead, maybe you slipped into thinking about something you did yesterday or want to do tomorrow. Maybe you were imagining what you would like to say to someone the next time you see him or her. When you begin to notice these thoughts you can try naming them: "That's a memory ... that's a fantasy ... I'm imagining ..." Don't dwell on analyzing these thoughts, just notice them, name them, and return to your sense perceptions and awareness of feelings in the present moment. Continue to ask yourself questions as a beginner's tool for noticing.

Becoming more skillful at noticing our distractions and emotions will help us to become more receptive to our loved ones as our focus on the present moment deepens. Through simple awareness exercises such as this one we become more able to offer our full presence to those with whom we are closest.

Nathaniel Shines the Light of Awareness

Simple awareness practice is important in our relationships with family because it is easy to slip into unconscious *reacting* to our loved ones rather than conscious *responding*. When things aren't going the way we want them to go, we may try to manipulate a situation or control or change our loved one through our words, our tone, or our body language. Often we are not even aware that we are doing it. Our efforts to control and manipulate come from the shadow places inside us, and if we don't notice it about ourselves, sometimes a loved one can help us see it.

This happened to me when I was living with a dear friend and her son, Nathaniel. When he was young, I gave Nathaniel weekly drum lessons. He had a straightforward innocence about him, but he sure could be frustrating! One day during a lesson he continually ignored my requests to refrain from playing the drum *while* I was talking to him. In this case, I do think he was getting a little pleasure from getting my goat. I tried to speak calmly to him. I tried to identify consequences for his actions. But nothing worked and my frustration grew and grew, until I began acting coldly toward him. I turned my body away from him more; I stopped smiling at him. I didn't even look at him as much, avoiding eye contact and simply going through the motions of the drum lesson.

Finally, this got his attention, and in that precious, childlike way he asked me, "Don't you love me anymore, Nanette?" This response truly stunned me. For a split second I saw myself through the eyes of this child, and saw how I was behaving by contracting my spirit into a tiny space, withholding my attention, withholding true human presence, human contact, as a means of punishing him. I saw myself through his eyes, and I saw myself in a clearer way than I ever had before. I realized that this was something I did with those I was close to—withholding love to make a point, to express anger or frustration. As the light of awareness flooded in, my heart melted. I turned my body toward him and directly addressed him, looking into his eyes, trying to explain in age-appropriate language how I felt. "I do love you," I said. "I'm just very frustrated because it seems you're not listening to me."

Awareness changed everything in this situation, and I became able to respond with compassion rather than react with anger. Without awareness, I was captive to my own unacknowledged feelings. The light of awareness shone in two directions in this experience. On the one hand, I had become aware of my feelings, accepted them compassionately, and made a choice to no longer be controlled by them. In that way, I had taken the focus off of him and the things about him that I couldn't control, and placed the focus back on me and the things that I could control—my actions and responses. On the other hand, and very significantly, I became aware of how my actions affected Nathaniel. Awareness allowed me to step outside the swirl of strong emotions and be more fully present with him. Awareness allowed me to detach from my feelings enough to see them, instead of being consumed and controlled by them.

Honestly, I can't remember his response to my explanation for my actions and my tone, or how we got through the rest of the drum lesson. But I will never forget what I learned about myself from him on that day. Somehow he broke through to me or I was ready to understand that I could express my anger and frustration without withholding love. I could express my disappointment without implying that he was not important to me, without signaling that I disliked who he was as a person, without being inhospitable. What I had done with him was disconnect; it was the opposite of receptivity, reverence, and generosity. I had withdrawn and was not emotionally present with him. What Nathaniel had done, without knowing he was doing it, was shine a light of awareness into the situation. He provided an opportunity to step back into the process of hospitality, which I did when I turned toward him with willingness to engage. This didn't mean that our problems were solved, but it did enable me to be authentically present and work toward improving the situation rather than tearing at the very foundation of our relationship by acting like I didn't love him.

I was lucky that Nathaniel had the youthful innocence and sincerity to ask the direct question, "Don't you love me anymore?" It is perhaps more common for family members to react in kind, withdrawing in reaction to withdrawal, or getting angry or afraid. We can't control the degree of self-awareness that family members bring to our relationships, but we can control ourselves. Noticing how our feelings affect us and how our actions affect others is the first step of hospitality because this awareness makes us available for relationship. It brings us to the present moment and we become receptive to others, holding an invitational and open posture.

DEVELOP ACCEPTANCE TO FOSTER REVERENCE

Reverence is an attitude or posture of active welcome. You can't force a feeling of reverence; you can't *will* yourself to feel reverent. But you can seek to be accepting in a compassionate way, and this will begin to foster reverence. As with awareness, acceptance is something to be practiced toward yourself as well as toward others. The two practices are intertwined, because compassionate acceptance of yourself and your thoughts and feelings will help prepare you to be compassionately accepting and reverent toward others.

Referring to our in-with-out concept, reverence is the "with" phase, the welcoming phase. In a state of reverence we stand in the full presence of another, being fully present ourselves. We seek to perceive the image of God in them, their inherent value and preciousness in the grand scheme of things. If you are currently living with family members, you can begin to practice this any time that you are in the presence of your family. If you are currently living alone, one way that you can practice this is as a kind of meditation, by holding your loved one in mind. You can also plan to practice the next time you are in the presence of your family.

- Begin with noticing. Acceptance flows from awareness; reverence flows from receptivity. Notice that your partner, spouse, child, sibling, or parent is alive, in a body, present with you. This is something of a miracle in and of itself. Really notice it.
- Reverence for family members means encountering them as they really are, without trying to change or control them. If you feel a desire to change them, if you feel irritated or frustrated by what they are doing, notice that, name it, and then let it go, returning to the awareness of their presence in your life, at the breakfast table, on the living room couch, in the backyard, or in

your bed. Be here now. Can you let Michael be Michael,
Sarah be Sarah, David be David, Karen be Karen?

- Ask yourself, "Who is this person?" You may think you
  know your family members because you have spent so
  much time with them, but do you really know what
  they love, what they fear, or what brilliant unique gifts
  they bring to the world? These questions are an invitation to perceive the mystery and blessing of your loved
  ones. It is a way of seeking the Life of life, or the image
  of God in them.
- Give the benefit of the doubt to family members that
  they are doing the best they can. This kind of trust is a
  great gift and expresses deep acceptance of each person
  as he or she is.
- Offer second chances to family members so that they
  (and you) can change and grow. Because family relationships span such long periods of time, you will probably have lots of opportunities to express compassionate
  acceptance in this way.
- When your loved ones tell you what is important to
  them, believe them. Especially when you disagree, try
  to really understand that they are different from you
  and that is okay. Don't try to turn them into you.
  Accept them as who they are. Love them for that.

Reverence is based on honesty and transparency, and no matter
how your loved one is acting, you can still choose to be honest
yourself. You may need to reach deep inside yourself and rely on
the fruits of hospitality to God and self, but you can do it nevertheless. When we are dwelling in reverence, we are seeking to be
in authentic relationships with real people. This means we have
to be authentic and honest about our experience, thoughts, and
feelings. Reverence is based on compassionately accepting people
as they really are and not trying to change or control them.

This can be especially difficult when we see our loved ones harming themselves. In some cases, we may feel a strong desire to look the other way, to dampen our awareness of *what is* because the situation is painful. When you find yourself denying or resisting what you perceive in your family relationships, then you are not compassionately accepting what is happening. This makes it truly difficult to be reverent and welcoming of the people you love. There is a natural tendency to deny and resist things that we don't want to be true. It's natural, it's forgivable, but it's not the most helpful. For example, it is difficult to acknowledge and accept when a loved one develops an addiction to alcohol or other drugs. But acceptance does not mean that you have to encourage or submit to whatever is happening; it means that you have to realize what is happening before you are able to respond to it. Acceptance of what is means that when you choose to respond, you are actually responding to what is really happening, rather than to what you wish were happening. Sometimes being hospitable means walking away from a situation because that is the only way to honor integrity and the inherent value of yourself or your loved one.

When your family situation gets tough, hospitality to yourself and your loved ones might include getting help in dealing with whatever is going on. That's a practical matter. Spiritually, practicing receptivity, reverence, and generosity toward yourself, your loved ones, and God, the source of love and life, can help lead you to wholeness through whatever journey you are on. Practicing deep hospitality is not always easy, but it is transformative.

PRACTICING REVERENCE WITH CHILDREN

The children in our families present unique opportunities for us to practice reverence. Because we are responsible for their formation and their safety, it is fairly easy to slip into a desire to control them. Extending hospitality to them, however, means learning to set appropriate boundaries while maintaining reverence in our relationships with them.

Henri Nouwen calls children "our most important guests, who enter into our home, ask for careful attention, stay for a while and then leave to follow their own way." He describes the kind of home that families can create for children so that they experience and grow in hospitality. A home that is hospitable to children is a place where "children can ask questions without fear and can experiment with life without taking the risk of rejection. There they can be encouraged to listen to their own inner selves and to develop the freedom that gives them the courage to leave the home and travel on."[2] Children need clear boundaries in order to feel safe, but they also need to feel loved to feel safe.

Once, two of my nieces were staying with me for a couple of weeks. One afternoon, one of them was playing out in the garage where we had stacked a few bales of hay to use as mulch in our garden. Her sister brought it to my attention that she was unbundling the hay and scattering it throughout the garage. I went out to assess the damage. Seeing the hay unbaled and strewn everywhere, I felt out of control of my environment, my own garage, my own hay. I asked my niece what she was doing, and she explained that she was using the hay to mark off different areas in her imaginary playhouse. I saw in her face and heard in her tone a vulnerability. I could tell she was scared about my reaction, and yet there was an innocent excitement about her game. She was happy about her imaginary scenario. With that awareness, I accepted as valuable her experience of the hay, which was quite different from mine, and allowed it to fill my awareness. I responded from that sense of connection with her experience and said, gently but firmly, "It was a good idea, but we need to keep the hay in the hay bales so it's ready to be used in the garden." She seemed to accept this quite readily and set about cleaning up the garage as I asked.

Later that day, she was describing the whole experience to another family member and her face lit up as she repeated, "It was a good idea!" The boundary she crossed in pulling apart the hay bales was one that she crossed innocently, not intending to create harm. She was experimenting with the world, with life, and with her imagination. What struck me about her retelling of the story was how clearly she needed the simple affirmation that she had a good idea!

Hospitality to children includes providing a receptive, reverent, and generous space in which they are free to be childlike, needy, creative, and messy at times. They are exploring their world and relationships, and they need the freedom to be explorers. Zen teacher Shunryu Suzuki said, "Even though you try to put people under some control, it is impossible. You cannot do it. The best way to control people is to encourage them to be mischievous. Then they will be in control in its wider sense. To give your sheep or cow a large, spacious meadow is the way to control him."[3] Doing this with children is offering them a safe space in which their creativity and development are received in a respectful and loving way by parents and other caretakers (like aunts!). Who they are and who they are becoming is a mystery and a blessing that we can hold in reverence. When we set respectful boundaries without trying to control children, we allow them to be the unique individuals they are. With this kind of reverence we can welcome them in their fullness and nurture their development through the third step of hospitality—generosity.

CHOOSE ACTIONS TO EMBODY GENEROSITY

Generosity transforms receptivity and reverence into a complete expression of hospitality. It is the "out" of in-with-out, and is an expression of compassionate love and grace. Generosity sometimes flows out of us very naturally, but often it requires an active choice to act differently than our initial impulse might suggest. In families, it is especially difficult to be generous when we feel very vulnerable or particularly attached to certain out-comes. In the hay-bale incident, for example, I was very attached to a tidy garage. When I lost control of that I had a choice between reacting with anger or responding with generosity. What made my generosity sincere and not self-depleting was my awareness of my niece's experience (a joyful game) and my acceptance that her experience was valuable. Receptivity and reverence allowed me to act with generosity.

A friend of mine, Ginny, undertook an interesting experiment in generosity with her mom, after having done a lot of self-examination regarding that formative relationship. She had been looking into her upbringing and her feelings about the ways in which she was limited by her past relationships with her parents. In particular, her mom had taken up residence inside her head as a critical voice. Whenever she was doing something, she would often imagine the criticism that her mother would have for her. She became aware that all she wanted was her mother's love and she felt she never got it. She accepted this as the way things were, which led her to wonder if her mom had a similar unmet need. This allowed her to broaden her awareness beyond the limitation of her own self, and become attentive (receptive) to and compassionately accepting (reverent) of her mother's experience as well.

Once she became aware and accepting on this level, she was able to come up with an idea and make a decision about an action of nurture that she wanted to take. It was an experiment really, an experiment in generosity with love. She decided she would send her mom a present every month for a whole year. The effects were very interesting. Every month, my friend told me, when she picked out a present to send her mom, she would hear all the criticisms her mom might have about that gift—all the ways it wasn't perfect or wasn't something that she would like or use, or how it could be better.

First, my friend just sat with this. She expanded her awareness and invited her full authentic self to show up, messy feelings and all. She noticed and watched all these thoughts and feelings rise up inside her, and recognized that her mother didn't even need to say any of these things to her, because now she was saying them to herself. The whole present scheme, she says now, was worth it just for this insight. By watching her own thoughts for a year like this, she was able to more easily identify those times she began criticizing herself (purportedly on behalf of her mom, or in her mom's voice), and she realized she didn't have to do that! By applying awareness and compassionate acceptance, she was able to make different choices about her actions toward herself.

To simply blame the self-critical voice on her mom wouldn't really get her out of the critical thinking, it would just reinforce and redirect the critical thoughts away from herself and back at her mom. But her mind would still be filled with critical and judgmental thoughts. Instead, she made a decision that whenever she noticed this critical voice coming up, she would name and accept that it was in her, and replace it with kind and generous thoughts about herself and her mother.

The giving of the gift, in fact, became a way for her to express hospitality, love, and caring for her mom, in spite of the critical voice. The gift giving undermined the power of the critical voice and reinforced a message of unconditional love. I asked her how this affected her relationship with her mom. "It's made us closer," she said. "There's more of an awareness and acceptance of the love between us now." In a way, what my friend did was create and reinforce an experience of unconditional love. Her decision to embody her love in generous ways transformed her, her mom, and their relationship.

HOSPITALITY PRACTICES WITH FAMILY

Practicing *awareness*, *acceptance*, and *action* will always move us in the direction of *receptivity*, *reverence*, and *generosity*. So it's helpful to use these practices as a kind of touchstone that we return to again and again. There is receptivity in the simple awareness of being present, together, here and now. This kind of deep presence is so precious that the mere fact of it occurring can create between you and your loved ones a feeling of mystery and joy. This is the essence of reverence—it is love, honor, respect, and tenderness. Once reverence arises in you, generosity flows out naturally. We want to express our care for those we love.

The gift of full attention is a powerful one that will make hospitality grow in you and flourish in your family. My very best memory of my grandfather is from one time when he looked me in the eyes with full attention. I must have been about four or five years old because I was little enough for him to pick me up by the waist and set me on the edge of the dining room table. There he played a game with me. He said, "I bet I can make you blink just by looking at you." I was very certain that I could resist his will and hold my eyes open forever. And so the contest began, me sitting on the dining room table, legs dangling over the edge, him standing in front of me. As the urge to blink grew bigger and bigger in me, I opened my eyes wider and wider and began to tilt my head slightly forward as though the angle of my head would help my eyes stay open. Eventually, of course, I blinked.

"Aha!" he teased. "You blinked! I knew I could make you do it!" With a big smile and a joking haughty attitude I told him that he didn't make me blink; I only blinked because I wanted to. He laughed and picked me up again by the waist and stood me back on the floor. "Now you'll blink all the time," he said. And it was true; I did. And for the longest time I believed that I had never blinked before my grandfather made me do it.

In that exchange with him, I knew that I was loved. He invited, welcomed, and nurtured me in an attentive, loving, and generous way. That was the gift he gave me, a form of hospitality expressed through giving me his deep presence and full attention. This is something that you can do with your family in innumerable ways. If you would like to begin developing this, here are just a few ideas to help you practice hospitality toward your family:

Try instituting regular signs of affection to be shared with family members. I have a friend whose husband brings her a red rose every single Friday night. This is one of the things they do to welcome in the Jewish Sabbath. Even if they've had a fight, he brings her a rose. There will always be time to continue the fight after the Sabbath is over, but the rose comes as a sign of commitment to love. This, too, is a form of hospitality: to remain receptive, reverent, and generous to a loved one, even when it requires consistency that feels bigger than us, even when we feel angry or hurt or particularly vulnerable. Vulnerability creates intimacy if we treat each other with respect and tenderness.

Practice talking to your family members in intentional ways. It's surprising how little we really do this. Find out what's important to them, what they spend time mulling over as they are about to drift off to sleep at night. Ask questions. Act interested. You might be amazed at how this simple added effort can make a big difference.

Be generous in sharing yourself, naming your needs and desires honestly. Be clear and direct to the best of your ability, saying what is true for you instead of expecting your loved ones to know intuitively what is important to you.

Set aside consistent, quality time *to be* together, not just *to do* together. This might be time for dinner, trips to the park, going to the movies, or just sitting around on the porch or in the living room. Are there games your family might like to play? We're so used to being busy all the time that this might be more difficult to do than it sounds. If you can enlist the commitment of at least one other family member, you may have better luck actually pulling it off. Even if no one else joins you at first, your having fun might begin to attract greater attention and participation.

Try the once-a-month gift-giving experiment, especially if you're struggling with a particular relationship. You can tell the recipient of your gifts what you plan to do, or you can just start doing it and see how long it takes the person to ask you what you're doing! As you go through the process, be intentional about becoming aware of your feelings and making decisions about how to respond to them. Remain aware, also, of the preferences, feelings, and desires of the person you are giving gifts to. Be sure to give presents that he or she is likely to enjoy, rather than gifts that you *wish* the person would enjoy. If you don't know what the person might enjoy, that is part of the marvelous adventure! Now you have to be an undercover detective and find out. Ask questions about what she enjoys, what she wishes for, or what she used to do but now misses. Conversation can go a long way toward identifying potential gifts.

Receptivity and reverence go hand-in-hand for this practice, since giving another person what he would enjoy requires becoming aware of what he might like, as well as honoring his desires and his personality with respect. This is what makes the action generous: grounding it in awareness and acceptance of the other person. It will be interesting to see how this kind of persistent focus on expressing your care for a person changes you and changes your relationship.

HOSPITALITY FROM HOME

As we cultivate hospitality within our families, we create homes that can become refuges for people in need. Christine Pohl, in her book about the history and practice of hospitality in Christian tradition, wrote "We should never trivialize the importance of welcoming family and friends into a loving place. Grace-filled hospitality to a relative or friend who needs some time and a place to recover from weariness or wounds is a tremendous gift."[4] I certainly experienced this on the receiving end when my friend took me in after a major life change that left me grieving and I needed a place to stay. As I mentioned earlier, she offered me her newly renovated writing studio in the attic, where I was able to live and heal for a year.

Shortly after I moved into my friend's attic I remember sitting on the floor around the coffee table with her family and a few close friends for Hanukkah celebrations. We were writing down all the things we could think of that we were grateful for and posting them on the walls all around the room. Everybody was laughing, but inside I was grieving. I felt like the wind had been knocked out of me; I had no air in my lungs. I saw and heard and participated in everything that was happening as though my whole body, mind, and heart were wrapped in gauze. It all seemed a bit muted, a bit distant. But I felt the vitality and the love there. I heard the children laughing. And I felt hope in that. I thought, *life goes on*, and love goes on, and human connection goes on. I searched around inside myself for things that I was grateful for, and my friend and her family were at the top of the list. For a while, they became my chosen family, and I became part of theirs. They had created a home into which they could welcome me and in which I could heal.

We can't have a life without challenges, pain, and disappointment. But we can have a life filled with real human relationships, deep love, and respect that lead to satisfaction and joy. For most of us, this begins with the family, with all its shortcomings and special joys. Coming to be at "home" within the self, drawing from the deep well of God's love, and practicing awareness, acceptance, and action, we find our relationships with our family strengthened. Extending hospitality to our loved ones helps us deal with the very real vulnerability that love requires of us. Letting go of the illusion of control, creating spacious but bounded contexts in which to explore the world and each other, and becoming attentive, present, and available to our loved ones—these are but some of the ways we extend hospitality to our families. Families, in turn, by creating homes filled with openness, love, and graciousness, can offer that hospitality back to the world.

HOSPITALITY TO NEIGHBORS

Becoming the Merciful Neighbor

When I was a newcomer to a neighborhood meditation center located in someone's home, I had an experience that
transformed my understanding of hospitality. After the first
meditation program that I attended there, we all gathered in the
somewhat small dining room, about fifteen of us, for tea and
snacks. As can happen in these kinds of situations, people began
chatting with the people they knew. However, I didn't know
anyone. I stood there awkwardly, feeling a bit miffed that no one
was speaking to me.

Didn't they realize that I was a newcomer? Couldn't they
see that I was feeling shy? Why wasn't anyone welcoming me? I
was assuming that they all felt secure and confident because they
"belonged." I thought I was the one who didn't belong, that I
was the outsider and therefore the one who needed to be welcomed. I even had a sense of entitlement about this. They *should
be* welcoming me. They *should be* aware of my vulnerabilities.

Finally, one of the hosts noticed me and introduced me to
someone else. As I began to talk and visit, I began to see that the

"regulars" felt just as vulnerable meeting me as I felt meeting them. Their body language told me that they were nervous. The pauses in our conversation allowed me to see that they didn't know what to say to me. As I became more aware of their experience, I metaphorically stepped outside myself into the space between us. In that space, I gently held their vulnerability along with my own. I stopped judging it and simply accepted it compassionately.

I suddenly understood that I had the power to be hospitable and neighborly *toward them*, even though I was new to their circle, the so-called outsider coming in. Realizing that I had this power meant I had to give up my "innocent victim" role and take responsibility for contributing a sense of warmth and hospitality to the situation. This interesting change in perspective was a shift from focusing on my vulnerability and the power of others to realizing my own power and the vulnerability of others. I noticed that I impacted those around me, either negatively by being withdrawn and insecure (disguised as "shy") or positively by being friendly and taking the risk to reach out and connect. This was immensely empowering, because I saw that I have the power to be hospitable in any situation. With this awareness, I could reach deeply inside myself and bring out the receptivity, reverence, and generosity that I have to offer.

My experience in that tiny room changed as I let go of judgment and closed-heartedness, and instead became receptive. My *awareness* expanded as I more accurately perceived the situation. When I saw their own vulnerabilities, just like mine, a kind of tenderness and *compassionate acceptance* rose up in me, which made it seem natural to act with kindness and *generosity*. Again, the hospitality in this experience had the same basic movement of in-with-out—and it's something you can practice by using your own power to apply awareness, develop acceptance, and act generously.

THE GOOD SAMARITAN WAS NEIGHBORLY

The well-known story of the Good Samaritan in the New Testament takes up this idea of being neighborly.[1] In the passage that introduces the story, a lawyer asks Jesus what he should do to gain the life of the age to come.[2] Jesus confirms what the lawyer has read in Hebrew scriptures: "You shall love God with all your heart, and with all your soul, and with all your strength, and with all your mind; and your neighbor as yourself." Jesus says to the lawyer, "Do this, and you shall live."

But the lawyer isn't satisfied by this answer. "And who is my neighbor?" he asks, looking for loopholes, probing the question of just whom he should love. Jesus answers with the story of the Good Samaritan. "There was a man," he says, "going down to Jerusalem from Jericho." Along the way, the man (who was presumably Jewish) is assaulted by robbers, stripped, beaten, and left for dead in the ditch. A Jewish priest passes by and doesn't help him, then a temple assistant (a Levite) passes by and doesn't help him. Finally, a stranger happens by—a foreigner, a man from Samaria. He pulls the injured man out of the ditch, cleans and bandages his wounds, takes him to an inn and spends two days' wages to put him up there, promising to pay the innkeeper even more when he comes back to check on the man.

Then, to drive the point of the story home, Jesus answers the lawyer's question "and who is my neighbor?" with a question of his own: "Who was the neighbor to the man in the ditch?" Jesus turns things upside down—although the lawyer asks, "*Who* is my neighbor," Jesus responds by describing what a neighbor *does*. He takes the emphasis off the identity of the other and places the responsibility on us to act in a neighborly way. The lawyer answers that the neighbor is the one who showed mercy, and Jesus says, "Go and do likewise." No loopholes. Jesus doesn't tell the lawyer who his neighbors are; Jesus tells the lawyer that he must *be* the neighbor.

Go, and do—this is how we become neighbors, by being active and not passive, by going toward and responding to those who come into our path with generosity and compassion. A neighbor is someone who is open to encounter, who responds with respect and takes real action. In these ways, a neighbor embodies the active receptivity, reverence, and generosity that make up hospitality.

GOD—SELF—NEIGHBOR: INTERBEING

In Christian tradition, the very nature of God is understood to demonstrate deep relationality. Orthodox Christianity describes the unity of the Trinity as *perichoresis*, an intimate dance between the three "persons" of the Trinity.[3] *Perichoresis* is a Greek word made by combining the root words *peri* and *choreio*, and means to move or dance around. It's trying to express the idea that God is one, and singular, and yet God is never solitary. The poetic beauty of *perichoresis* is the suggestion that God is forever dancing with God's self—an expression of joyful love-centered withness. God is always in relationship. It is a paradoxical idea reflecting the mystery of unity in diversity and diversity in unity. As human beings created in the image of God, we also exist in this mysterious, interconnected yet differentiated way, and hospitality as a spiritual practice calls us to awareness of this deep relationality.

A similar concept is found in other spiritual traditions. Vietnamese Buddhist monk Thich Nhat Hanh has a word for this deep relationality: *interbeing.*[4] A flower, for example, is made up of the relationship between sun, rain, and earth. The flower is the flower, but the flower is also earth, rain, and sun literally intermixing to become and to be the flower. Earth, rain, and sun exist within the flower—they inter-be. The different elements exist intermingled with one another, separate and yet making a new singular thing. We humans are like that flower, too, inter-existing with other humans, with all of creation, and with the God in whom "we live and move and have our being."[5] Zen master Shunryu Suzuki describes something similar: "Each existence depends on something else. Strictly speaking, there are no separate individual existences. There are just many names for one existence."[6]

This mysterious idea of interbeing is very relevant to hospitality because it has to do with accurately perceiving our relationships with others. Thomas Merton saw from this interconnected place when he had his famous street-corner epiphany. "In Louisville, at the corner of Fourth and Walnut, in the center of the shopping district, I was suddenly overwhelmed with the realization that I loved all those people, that they were mine and I theirs, that we could not be alien to one another even though we were total strangers. It was like waking from a dream of separateness."[7]

In reflecting on his experience, Merton described the experience of waking from the dream of separation as freeing: "This sense of liberation from an illusory difference was such a relief and such a joy to me that I almost laughed out loud."[8] He realized that being a monk didn't make him fundamentally different from other human beings. He had a deep experience of belonging to the human family, of being the *same* on some fundamental level. His monastic solitude prepared him to have this experience, but he realized that even in his receptive solitude he was not separate from others, but always deeply interconnected. "It is because I am one with them that I owe it to them to be alone, and when I am alone, they are not 'they' but my own self."[9]

Merton's vocation was to be a solitary monk and he found ways to extend hospitality and to serve people from his own context. Most of us, however, don't live in monasteries but instead live in towns, cities, and neighborhoods. Merton's insight into the unity underlying difference has relevance to us because understanding that we inter-exist with others changes how we think about being neighbors and extending hospitality. Neighbors aren't a "them" separate from an "us." It suggests that hospitality to others is an expression of hospitality to the self and to God.

Oneness and Variety Are the Same Thing

In addition to Merton's perception of his unity with the people all around him at the corner of Fourth and Walnut, he also saw the unique beauty in the diversity of the people. Merton wrote, "Then it was as if I suddenly saw the secret beauty of their hearts, the depths of their hearts where neither sin nor desire nor self-knowledge can reach, the core of their reality, the person that each one is in God's eyes. If only they could all see themselves as they really *are*. If only we could see each other that way all the time. There would be no more war, no more hatred, no more cruelty, no more greed.... I suppose the big problem would be that we would fall down and worship each other. But this cannot be *seen*, only believed and 'understood' by a peculiar gift."[10]

While we look for the humanity we share, we might be tempted to overlook the beautiful differences that Merton was describing. Suzuki warns against overemphasizing oneness to the detriment of acknowledging diversity. "Oneness is valuable," he says, "but variety is also wonderful. Ignoring variety, people emphasize the one absolute existence, but this is one-sided understanding. In this understanding there is a gap between variety and oneness. But oneness and variety are the same thing, so oneness should be appreciated in each existence. That is why we emphasize everyday life rather than some particular state of mind. We should find the reality in each moment, and in each phenomenon."[11]

Suzuki brings us back to the foundational step of hospitality, awareness in everyday life. Practicing awareness and noticing everyday details imbues life with vitality as we become more fully connected to what is right in front of us—people, our relationships, our thoughts and emotions, our environment. Awareness practice will help us hold lightly the tension between unity and diversity, variety and oneness.

BEING A NEIGHBOR MAKES A DIFFERENCE

Sometimes we might wonder just how much good our hospitality can do in the world. Will what I do make a dent in any of the world's problems? It's easy to think that it won't, that our tiny efforts don't matter. If we get stuck in this perspective, though, it can lead us to give up our very real power to make a difference in people's lives.

This dilemma was dramatically portrayed in the movie *Hotel Rwanda*,[12] which tells the true story of Paul Rusesabagina, a man who was living a fairly successful life as a hotel manager in Rwanda before a devastating genocide began there. In one scene, in an intimate conversation with his wife, he tells her that he can only take care of his own family; he can't be concerned about the other families that are in danger. But what Paul learned through his later experiences is what we all must learn eventually: our survival is wrapped up with the survival of others.

Paul's isolationalist way of thinking was challenged when he found himself, his family, and his neighbors captives of the militia, all of them about to be executed in the street. Paul began to negotiate with their captors, attempting to buy his family's freedom through bribery. His neighbors looked at him with pleading and terror in their eyes and he realized that he couldn't, in the end, abandon them willingly. His worldview expanded in that moment, and his care and concern grew to embrace a much larger circle of humanity. As he negotiated to save the lives of his family members, he also negotiated to save the lives of all the people there with him. After a harrowing escape from this crisis, Paul went on to save the lives of as many people as he could fit into his hotel for protection.

Paul's story may seem larger than life because the situation of genocide is so very extreme and because his story has been told on the big screen. This might make him seem like he himself is larger than life, or that we could never be like him. But, in truth, we can be like him. He responded as a good neighbor responds

to the people who come into her or his presence. He found compassion and strength within himself to care for more people than
he thought he could care for. We can do the same.

Sometimes the neediness of our neighbors, their hunger,
their suffering, or the powers oppressing them, seem too large
and overwhelming for us. But it is often our sense of inability
to change everything that prevents us from changing anything. Mother Teresa talked about the importance of doing
the things that might seem small but will nevertheless have a
deep impact. "We ourselves feel that what we are doing is just
a drop in the ocean. But if that drop was not in the ocean, I
think the ocean would be less because of that missing drop. I
do not agree with the big way of doing things. To us what
matters is an individual. To get to love the person we must
come in close contact with him."[13] It takes great love to step
outside our fear and self-protectionism, into a space of generosity. What we don't often realize is that taking just one
step outside our isolationism to help our neighbors, even one
act at a time, has the power to transform us completely. The
transformation takes place on its own when we take the risk
of opening our hearts and approaching others, of letting them
get close to our hearts.

Homan and Pratt write about this in their book *Radical
Hospitality*. The little acts of kindness we do "push at the great
big darkness, the darkness that is so huge we feel helpless and so
we do nothing and try to make ourselves feel good about it. This
is a heart problem. We don't lack resources or opportunity, we
lack heart."[14] When we allow ourselves to do nothing because
we can't do everything, we demonstrate this "heart problem" by
failing to see and come close to the people that we can help.

My own faith community, for example, is helping a family
of three go through a program that assists them in becoming
housed after being homeless. It's a drop in the bucket of homelessness, but it makes a difference to this one mom and her two

kids. It also helps us grow more neighborly and compassionate, because it makes the problem of homelessness a real problem for us, associated with real people. We can't look the other way as easily, once we begin to know the actual individuals, their faces, their families, their situations. Really knowing and caring for people may inspire us to join together with others so that we can make a bigger impact on social problems. But our impact will be greatest if it begins with and is filled with receptivity, reverence and generosity toward actual people. When we begin to get to know people, they become the people in our path and we become their neighbors, just as the Samaritan man became the neighbor of the wounded man. That certainly made a difference to the beaten man lying in the ditch.

Go Out to Come Near—Expand Your Neighborly Awareness

The English word *neighbor* comes from the Old English meaning a *near dweller*, one who dwells nearby. And yet, the neighbor in the Good Samaritan story is the stranger, the foreigner, the traveler passing through. This underscores that neighborliness does not have to do with where one lives but has more to do with how one lives. Although the Samaritan did not *live near* the wounded man, he allowed himself to *come near* the man. The Good Samaritan lived with an open heart and a commitment to compassion. He lived with a sense of relationality with those who came into his path.

The Good Samaritan story is even more powerful because it shows how socially constructed physical and cultural barriers did not stop the Samaritan, who would have been considered an enemy of Jews at that time, from loving and serving the person who needed his help. To extend neighborly hospitality means becoming a neighbor by coming near to those who differ from us. This can be a great way to expand our awareness and embody our invitation and receptivity to neighbors.

What follows are a few ideas to help you think about changing the habits and patterns of your life to become a more aware, accepting, and generous neighbor.

- **Visit neighborhoods other than your own.** Find neighborhoods with cultural influences different than your own, where you will encounter people and practices that seem unfamiliar to you. Simply go for a walk there and notice the people, the art, the colors, the architecture, the activities, the places where people gather. Eat a meal, go to an event, look for the "secret beauty" of the hearts of the people you encounter. Think of them as sisters and brothers in your family. How does this idea change you?

- **Notice the people who *do* live near you.** Consider how you could be more aware and respectful and generous toward them. You might begin by simply saying hello. Find out the names of your neighbors and tell them yours. Perhaps you could tell them something about yourself to begin to establish a small connection with them—have you noticed anything you have in common? At some point, you might be able to invite them to your house for coffee, a group dinner, or a party.

- **Practice *awareness, acceptance, action* in unfamiliar places.** Notice feelings of uncertainty, fear, shame, and anxiety that may come up when you are in an unfamiliar place where you may not understand the traditions or cultural expectations. With accurate perception (awareness), you can find compassion (acceptance) for yourself and others. Once you experience this compassionate acceptance, you can choose how you want to express yourself and extend kindness and generosity (action) in this setting.

- **Look for unique beauty in those you meet.** Whom do you see when you look around? Do you see the uniqueness shining through each individual in some way? Look for that uniqueness—it will help you avoid boxing people into your projections, assumptions, and preconceived ideas.
- **Share daily life activities with a variety of people. For example, share meals with people you don't know.** People tend to hang out with people they know and people who are most similar to them. Look for opportunities to eat with people you wouldn't normally eat with. Go to an educational forum at a cultural center honoring a culture other than your own, or go to a community-building dinner for an advocacy organization. Some hospitality programs serve community dinners at which homeless and housed people sit down for dinner together. If this doesn't exist in your town or city, can you make it happen? It takes conscious effort to mix up our lives and intermingle more.
- **Expand the horizons of your "neighborhood" through reading and education.** Intentionally read books by people who are different from you in some way. Watch films that are popular in communities other than your own. Librarians are treasure troves of information on what's available. Through reading, we can "meet" people and gain insight and sensitivity, which can help us when we meet people face-to-face. Educating ourselves and expanding our horizons takes the pressure off of other people to educate us, and we can often become better conversation partners and better friends and allies to people who used to be strangers to us.
- **Learn another language.** Learning another language can teach you two things. Specifically, learning another language can help equalize the power imbalance in a

relationship in which conversation is held in the mother tongue of only one of the participants. More generally, it can also help us understand how frustrating it can be when you have something you really want to share or explore, but simply don't have the words to do it. Identifying with the challenges faced by others helps us get in touch with our compassion.

All of these practices can add new dimensions to your experience and change the shape and pattern of your life, developing in you tools you need to become more receptive, reverent, and generous with neighbors and in all your interactions.

COMPASSIONATE ACCEPTANCE—DAB MERCY ON YOUR JUDGING MIND

Sometimes we can get caught up in a whirlwind of judgmental thoughts that have the effect of separating us from neighbors and preventing us from truly encountering the beautiful unique-ness and honoring the mysterious oneness we share with others. If we allow these types of critical thoughts and negative feelings to shut us down toward others, then we are not able to create a receptive space in which to encounter them in their full human-ity, flaws and all. We're not able to act as kind and compassion-ate neighbors because we are either judging them or judging ourselves. Awareness, acceptance, and action can help us deal with this obstacle, but first, let's take a look at the problem.

Recently, several people have approached me in my capacity as pastor to talk about the difficulty they have in making friends. Everybody's story, of course, is unique. I do notice, however, some common experiences and underlying themes in many peo-ple's struggle with reaching out to others. Certain refrains recur with surprising regularity: "Nobody can understand me—I'm different" and "If people really knew me, they wouldn't like me." Or, on the other side of the coin, "I honestly don't like people very much … they're too shallow" (or selfish, or superficial, or whatever it is).

All three of these comments express judgmental and critical attitudes that keep our hearts tight and our love conditional. In the first two examples, the people are judging themselves as unknowable or unlikable. In the third case, the speaker is judging others as somehow unworthy of the effort, perhaps focusing on the "returns," measuring the value of what he or she might get out of the effort invested in getting to know people. By focusing on the "returns" or doubting the value of people around us, we can undermine our own desires to be connected or to make friends. We can also undermine our efforts to connect with people by doubting our own value and capacity to connect. Such judgments have the effect of separating us from people for unreal reasons.

If the Good Samaritan had been worried about the worthiness of the injured person in the ditch, he might have walked on by like the priest and temple assistant did. After all, Jews and Samaritans were considered enemies at that time. He might have looked in the ditch and seen someone he had been taught to despise and never to think of as worthy or as a neighbor at all. On the other hand, if he had doubted his own worthiness, he might have thought, well, my assistance won't make that much of a difference anyway—this problem is bigger than me. But the Good Samaritan didn't do any of those things; he was the one who showed mercy.

What a wonderful word: mercy. It makes me think of a line from *The Secret Life of Bees* by Sue Monk Kidd. The young protagonist of the book mentions those times in life when "somebody dabs mercy on your beat up life."[15] I think mercy is like that—something you can dab. We need to dab mercy a lot more often on ourselves and on all the people we encounter. How can we do that? How can we dab mercy?

Well, the first step is to look at the wound you want to dab. First you have to notice that you are judging in the negative sense—being overly and noncompassionately critical of yourself or others. Often I find that critical judgment of others lies on top of other more vulnerable emotions. For example, in the dining room at the neighborhood meditation center, when I became angry that people weren't actively welcoming me, there were other feelings hiding underneath my critical mind. I felt lonely. I felt afraid. I felt unlikable—all of which initially prevented me from being hospitable and neighborly myself. These are difficult feelings to notice because they make us feel more out of control, more vulnerable. They are tied to judging the self, not loving or accepting the self. It's easier and less painful to judge others than it is to see that we judge and dislike ourselves.

You can dab a little mercy on yourself just by making the space to notice this. Rather than being lost in the negative thinking, take a step back and notice that your thoughts are thoughts and that you're the one thinking them. They're things you're repeating in your mind, and you don't have to keep doing that. You are the actor in your life, and you have choices about how you act. And while you can't stop thinking, you can notice that you *are* thinking, and notice *what* you're thinking, and that will be the first step toward not being unconsciously controlled by your thoughts. This is the essence of awareness.

While you're at it, also notice the result that your critical and judgmental thoughts have on your life. Do they increase the level of isolation in your life, give you a sensation of powerlessness to change, or reinforce an image of yourself as a negative person? How are these thoughts affecting your life? Noticing these results can really be a wake-up call, and I hope it leads you to asking, "Do I really want to harbor these thoughts?" Harboring thoughts means protecting them, giving them permission to dock in your head and drop anchor. Sometimes we "give permission" by simply looking the other way, by not noticing that it's happening. Notice what you are thinking and the results those thoughts are having on your life, and you might decide you don't want to give these particular thoughts unlimited safe harbor.

But don't think that you are unique in having these struggles with a judging mind. Consider that you're just another bozo on the bus, as they say in some self-help programs. You're just another person on the corner of Fourth and Walnut. Accept the fact that you are perfectly human, negative thoughts and all. There is a secret beauty in the depth of your heart that God sees, just like in the hearts of all the other people standing on the corner. Even if you can't see that yet, dab mercy on your judging heart. And if you are seeing other people's flaws more than you are seeing your own, dab mercy on their hearts, too. That's step two of hospitality—acceptance in the form of mercy, mercy, mercy. The Good Samaritan was "the neighbor," according to Jesus; it wasn't the man in the ditch. The neighbor was the one who showed mercy.

This kind of mercy draws out of you a more unconditional love that allows you to complete the cycle of hospitality with generosity. The Samaritan showed generosity by taking the wounded man to an inn. You, too, can actively begin to be more kind, and you don't have to start in such dramatic ways. The smiles inside you might suddenly come out! You might turn to someone you don't know, smile, tell him your name, and ask his. Kindness. It's so simple, but it's so easy to forget to be generous in offering it.

EXPRESSIONS OF GENEROSITY—PUT HOSPITALITY INTO ACTION

To move into the third stage of hospitality, you have to first decide that you want to do it. To be generous is to be free—free of clinging to false security or to illusory control. It's not about being burdened with responsibility and it's not about acting the way you think you should act. The truth is, if you can tap into the generous spirit that is within you, you will be free because you will move away from clinging to your small life and your life will expand. Your world will become bigger because there will be more people and more relationships in it. There will be more love and mercy and discovery in your life as you engage with a wider variety of people and encounter the secret beauty in their hearts. There will also be less fear, less isolationism, and less self-obsession as you begin to let go of the idea that you can control life or protect yourself or your family from the risks of being fully alive and engaged with the world and the other people in it.

And this is where extending hospitality in a neighborly way becomes a spiritual discipline. To really know people takes time. To really hear and see people, to develop history and trust with them takes a commitment to changing the shape of our lives and prioritizing people. Being a good neighbor means being proactive and using your power to reach out and to invite others into relationship—at whatever level. That relationship might be a passing onetime conversation, or it might be the beginning of a long-term relationship in which you share your lives with each other more deeply.

One way to be a proactive neighbor is by fostering connections and creating opportunities for shared experiences among people. Get on the phone and call around, inviting a group of people to go canoeing, or to have a dinner gathering, or to visit an art gallery. Whatever the activity, let it be out of the normal scheme of busy, everyday life. Planning ahead can help a group of people make space and time for being together.

Consistency and commitment are important because they allow relationships to develop. I mentioned in chapter 1 how I used to celebrate Shabbat dinner with my Jewish housemates, our neighbors, and our friends every Friday night. There have been other times in my life when this kind of weekly gathering was important in maintaining and developing community connections. When I was in seminary in Chicago, a group of friends and I had a rotating dinner. Every week the same group of about ten people would get together at someone's apartment for dinner.

Being such a large group meant that people could miss the gathering when they needed to, but we enjoyed the get-together so much that we really tried not to. I think it was the highlight of the week for many of us. We rotated houses, and people cooked in pairs so the burden wasn't resting on the shoulders of any one individual. This meant that people who lived alone doubled up with a friend to cook together, another element of fun. Once we were all together, eating, we talked about what was going on in our week, what was coming up, and how we were feeling about it all. This kind of regular neighborly gathering is something that anyone can host, and it will go far toward creating deeper relationships.

INVITE PEOPLE INTO YOUR HOME ON A REGULAR BASIS

Do this once a month, once a week, four times a year. Here are some ideas to get you started.

- Invite a variety of individuals into your home to share meals at different times. Alternatively, invite the same groups of individuals repeatedly, to allow history and trust to develop within the group.
- Make the mealtime leisurely and simple. Don't try to entertain or impress them—just try to get to know them. It's the consistency and the commitment that allows deeper and deeper connections to develop over time. A smaller group (smaller than ten) might make it easier to talk deeply and honestly about life.
- Be intentional about conversation. One thing that we've found in my faith community is that without intentionality around conversation, we tend to fall easily into our default social mode, in which we try to keep our happy

faces on, and never really get to know each other in more significant ways.

GENEROSITY OF ATTENTION—MAKING INTENTIONAL CONVERSATION

Another much needed form of generosity in the world is the simple act of paying attention to others. Attentive listening seems to be a rare occurrence in our overly active and self-absorbed society. Actively inviting others to share themselves with us through conversation often feels like a big dab of mercy freely shared. Just think about a time when someone really seemed to take an interest in you, *in you*, and asked you all kinds of deep questions about yourself and the things that really matter to you. This is a gift that we can become more skillful in giving.

I first began to learn about the art of conversation from my college friend, Hannah, who wondered aloud why I never asked her any questions about herself. I told her that if she wanted me to know something about herself, she should just tell me. After all, that's the way it worked in my family of origin. But for Hannah, that's not how it worked at all. To her, my lack of initiating questions implied that I had no real interest in knowing her. It's not that I didn't care; I had absolutely no practice at proactively turning my attention toward someone else in that way. No one had ever modeled that kind of active communication and mutual discovery in my life.

So I began to watch how Hannah did it with other people. When she met someone, she asked them questions. "How long have you been doing this? Do you enjoy your job? What makes it difficult? What's your favorite food? Where do you go for fun?" Basically, she would invite people to share with her the most important and meaningful parts of themselves and their lives. People opened up around her. They felt cared for and felt connected. Her active and invitational listening created a safe space for people to be authentic and to break out of isolation and into community, into relationship.

Intentional conversation has just this effect of creating a free and open space between the people conversing. It is the space of encounter in which we are deeply attentive to each other. In this space, we foster our curiosity about each other and express that curiosity in the form of an invitation to know each other better. We invite another person to tell us who he or she is. Practicing intentional conversation means practicing how to communicate an active interest in the nitty-gritty day-to-day lives and experiences of other people. To practice with intentionality, we may have to reprioritize our lives so that we have time to know, time to inquire, and time to listen with rapt attention. We can practice intentional conversation when we are "going out to come near" as we explored earlier in this chapter. Offering generosity of attention can help us when we reach outside our comfort zones and strive to cross societal boundaries that keep us living in different neighborhoods, isolated homes, and effectively separate worlds.

As you prepare to practice intentional conversation, first consider what makes a conversation hospitable. Can you think of examples of times when you have felt deeply welcomed, heard, and valued in a conversation? What words go beyond the casual to create that sense of interrelatedness? And equally importantly, what body language conveys that you are truly available for an authentic conversation?

Second, ask yourself what interests you about people. Asking yourself this question will help you prepare to engage in conversation with authentic interest. To get at this, consider what interests you about the people you know and love best. Is it their activities? Is it their philosophical thoughts? Their fun nature? Their jokes? Their love of cooking? Their creativity in general? What do you think motivates them? What moves them most? What do they care most about? Answering these questions for yourself will give you ideas about areas to pursue with others in conversation. You might even want to jot down some of your responses to these questions to help you focus.

Third, reflect on your experience with conversation. What are the qualities of the most enjoyable conversations you've had? Were they fast and intense, over a cup of coffee or while walking down the street? Were they slow and leisurely over brunch? Did you pause a lot? Did you cover a lot of territory or just dive deeply into one topic? What kinds of conversations do you love to have? These questions can help you recognize and maximize your own style and passions in making conversation. Identifying your own interests and the pleasure you get from certain kinds of conversation will also awaken your curiosity about other people.

Finally, a fourth thing you can do to prepare for intentional conversation is to have a couple of good reliable questions on hand to get things going when your mind goes blank. I advise avoiding talking about the weather and what people "do" for a living, simply because these tend to be our social default questions, to which everyone tends to have default answers. Our social default is to stay pretty superficial, and intentional conversation is meant to undermine that tendency! Here are a few other possible conversation starters:

- **"What do you do for fun?"** can be a good starter, and also serve as a reminder to open up possibilities for fun. Someone asked me this just the other day, and my mind went blank. On the other hand, this caused me to think seriously about the fun in my life, and after we chatted for a while I started remembering the things I do that make me laugh.
- **"Do you have any hobbies?"** is another question that has been interesting to answer and to hear the answer to. You'd be amazed at some of the hobbies people do have. This is another way to get to the topic of "fun"

and how people relax—a topic we need to keep reminding each other about in our fast-paced world.

- **"What's been on your mind lately?"** is a nice open question. I like how open that is, because people can take it any number of ways, depending on how much attentiveness we offer them as listeners.

And the questions my college friend Hannah taught me, which I listed above, are also some good ones: "How long have you been doing this? Do you enjoy your job? What makes it difficult? What's your favorite food? Where do you go for fun?"

The idea is to invite people to share the *important* stuff in their lives with us, to offer an opportunity to go a little deeper than we usually do. So once you've got a conversation going, pay attention to the passions and interests that come out and follow up on those. Listen, listen, listen, and then ask a little bit more. Remember what you've learned and bring it up in later conversations so that you can go deeper. This also shows that your interest is sincere. Try it with your friends and family first, then try it with strangers and new acquaintances. You might find that when you extend the neighborly gesture of inviting deeper conversation, acquaintances more quickly become friends.

SMILE AND SAY HELLO

When I lived at a residential retreat center in the Catskill Mountains for five weeks, I was assigned a variety of ways to help out around the place. One of the best and most transformative things that I ever did there was to serve as welcomer at the front lobby. People came to the retreat center from all around the world, and they arrived day and night, having flown or taken trains or buses or taxis. Sometimes they arrived by car, having driven their station wagon full of kids and supplies for an extended stay in one of the family cottages. They came bedraggled and exhausted, anxious or exhilarated. Some didn't know what to expect, others came as old pros.

My role was to welcome them and help with initial orientation. I would tell them where to check in at registration, where to store their luggage temporarily, how the shuttle buses worked, where the dining room was, where the meditation hall was, when the evening program began, and then attempt to answer any number of assorted questions. That was very important and very helpful. But the most important thing I did, and the most transformative, was simply to take a deep breath and look them in the eyes, smile, and say hello.

This is the simple practice of being fully present with another human being. Why don't you try it? It includes shining the light of your awareness toward others, reverently welcoming them and generously giving the unconditional love that flows through you from a deeper source. The more you practice it, the more easily and naturally you will do it. So as you go through your day, take a deep breath, look into the eyes of those you meet, smile, and say hello. In that moment of greeting, drop everything else, drop every thought, drop every task. Breathe deeply to center yourself in your body and in the present moment. *Now*, in your *body*, you can look in the eyes of another, smile, and say hello. As simple as it seems, it's a generous and neighborly gift that will transform you in the giving and dab mercy on the life of someone you greet.

CHAPTER FIVE

HOSPITALITY TO STRANGERS

Pursuing Kinship Rather than Estrangement

Waiting in line for a community meal at a Chicago meditation center, I was talking with a young woman in line in front of me. She was outgoing, chatty, and enthusiastic. As we talked, I became aware of an older gentleman standing in line behind me, a quiet man, wearing a cotton summer hat pulled down low over his forehead. Seeing that he wasn't talking to anyone, I wanted to draw him into our conversation, so I introduced myself and began immediately practicing my skills of intentional conversation. With my body language, by turning first toward him, then toward the woman in front of me, I invited him into conversation with her as well. He surprised me by opening right up and speaking so movingly about spiritual practice and his own transformative experiences that within five minutes both of us listening to him had tears welling up in the corners of our eyes.

Taking a receptive posture and extending our hospitality to strangers often brings us an unexpected gift. In this case, as in so many cases, the greatest gift was the generous sharing of someone's authentic experience, a real encounter with another human being, heart to heart. Hospitality is about so much more than welcoming a stranger to our dinner table. It involves welcoming people into our lives, and welcoming their lives and stories into our hearts. Hospitality is fundamentally about our attitudes toward our fellow human beings, in which we realize that we are more deeply connected than estranged.

What keeps us from taking the risks necessary to realize this spiritual kinship we have with strangers? Sometimes it is fear of the unknown. After all, we don't know a stranger, and we can't be sure what will happen if we really open our hearts to him or her. We could be disappointed, shunned, rejected, or otherwise hurt. Taking the risk to welcome a stranger might mean escorting ourselves through our own fears so that we can come out on the other side of fear to the place of courage, openness, and relationship. We don't have to let fear stop us from becoming the kind of receptive, reverent, and generous people we want to become. Two other obstacles to experiencing the kinship of our common humanity are pridefulness and shame, which, as we shall see, turn out to be two sides of an egotistical mind-set that reinforces feelings of estrangement rather than connection.

Yet there is a particular blessing in welcoming strangers. It is often found precisely in opening up to the mystery of a stranger— taking a risk to sail into uncharted waters and see what we discover. There are different degrees of mystery around strangers, depending on the context of our interactions. Encountering complete strangers may carry more risk than engaging with strangers who are known in some way—a friend of a friend, for example, or a new colleague. Meeting people in the relative safety of a familiar context, such as a meditation center, a class, or a workplace, can also reduce the risk of engaging with them. But every encounter with a stranger carries with it uncertainty. If uncertainty and lack of control are difficult for you, your anxieties when meeting strangers may tempt you to withdraw, mistrust, and withhold—

the exact opposite of hospitality. Or you may express your anxiety by talking incessantly, thereby not allowing open space in which to truly encounter another person. Both withdrawal and overtalking are manifestations of non-receptivity and create distance between you and others. They are akin to pulling up the drawbridge to your life and flooding the moat around the fortress of your heart; when you do that, you find that you are all alone in that fortress. On the other hand, if you're able to keep your heart open, it becomes more like a living garden in which you can encounter and be changed by others, even strangers.

BEYOND FEAR—ENTERING THE GARDEN OF THE HEART

When we feel fearful or vulnerable due to things we cannot control, there is a tendency to clench the heart, to squeeze other people out of it. But when we trust the strength and integrity of our own hearts, we gain wisdom and compassion in the face of our own vulnerabilities. A trusting heart is a relaxed heart, free of fear. We trust that we are safe and will be well. The garden of such a heart where we can meet others has plenty of free and open space in it. Henri Nouwen calls this open space "poverty of heart." The poverty is the emptiness, the openness, the receptivity. "In a fearful environment it is not easy to keep our hearts open to the wide range of human experiences. Real hospitality, however, is not exclusive but inclusive and creates space for a large variety of human experiences."[1] Because it is a risk to step outside our comfort zones to engage people and places "strange" to us, sometimes even the safest environment can feel like a fearful one. We bring our fear with us. But holding our hearts open is something we can practice. We can exercise our heart muscles. Hospitality, Nouwen said, shouldn't be "limited to its literal sense of receiving a stranger in our house—although it is important never to forget or neglect that!—but as a fundamental attitude toward our fellow human being."[2]

So how can we exercise our heart muscles? We can practice taking risks and reaching out to people even when we're not sure how to do it. Sometimes it means going outside our comfort zones and opening our hearts despite the ways we've been taught to keep them tight and closed "for our own protection." Sometimes it means challenging our stereotypes and expectations. Often it means risking being imperfect, out of control, embarrassed, making a fool of ourselves, or just plain failing. But if we do it for heart reasons, for love, for hospitality, then our hearts will get stronger and stronger, so even if we do "fall down," the strength of our hearts will help us get back up again.

Recently I've started praying out loud in Spanish in my faith community as an expression of hospitality. English is my first language, and I've only studied Spanish a little bit, so I can only pray in Spanish if I have the words written down that I want to say. The first time I did this, I almost panicked and didn't do it. I had the words in front of me, and I thought, I don't have to say this. I can just say it in English. I was so afraid of mispronouncing the words that my heart began to race and my face got very flushed. I didn't want the embarrassment of saying things the wrong way, and I didn't want the Spanish speakers in my community to misunderstand me. I wanted them to feel that I was welcoming them, that I was making the effort to speak in a way that felt like home to them. I wanted to expand our English-speaking home into a more welcoming, more inclusive home.

I went through with it, stumbling over a couple of words, and feeling filled with fear and embarrassment. This was a very good feeling for me to have, I realized, because by passing through my fear, I found that I *can* pass through it. My fear doesn't have to stop me from doing the sometimes hard work of becoming hospitable. My intention was to do something to help Spanish speakers feel more welcomed into our faith community, but perhaps the real lesson was for me. Stepping outside the comfort zone of my mother tongue helped me better understand the experience of members of our community who have worked so hard to learn English as a second language. By making this effort, I was able to more deeply understand their frustration and discomfort when they don't know how to express themselves in *my* first language, English. By noticing and accepting my feelings, I escorted myself *through* my fear and embarrassment so that our space could become a bigger space, where we take risks together as a community. Sometimes smiling and saying hello is not enough. We can do more by taking the risk to learn about each other's experiences and to embrace our differences. Not just cultural differences, but also the differences between us as complex individuals with complex identities.

ESTRANGEMENT ARISES WHEN FEAR ARISES

Human beings are vulnerable. That's part of being human, and it's healthy to recognize and embrace this vulnerability. Where we get ourselves into trouble is when we try to deny our vulnerability and try to control things that cannot be controlled. For one thing, our hearts will be broken sometimes. People will let us down, and we will let ourselves down. Things out of our control will complicate our lives, from unexpected illnesses to catastrophic accidents. We can take appropriate steps to care for ourselves, of course, but things will happen that we cannot control or prevent, and sometimes it will hurt badly.

Having awareness and acceptance that vulnerability *is* part of life allows us to keep our eyes open, to see vulnerability within ourselves and within others, which allows us to perceive ourselves and each other more accurately. It's the beginning of hospitality, a way to prepare ourselves to be receptive. On the other hand, if we are frightened by vulnerability and try to deny or avoid it, we not only miss out on the exhilaration of much of life, but we are also more likely to push away the vulnerable strangers we encounter. Rather than letting our fear box us into a carefully conscribed life where we try to avoid vulnerability, we can step through and out of our fear into greater relationship. Paradoxically, by allowing ourselves to become more vulnerable, we tap into an inner source of love and trust, which helps us become more resilient in the face of things we fear.

In addressing our fear, we also begin to address the deep estrangement that is common in our culture. It is almost as though we live as strangers in a world full of strangers—we've become so isolated as individuals or small family units that a sense of community can be hard to come by. Henri Nouwen described the persistent alienation we see in our culture today: "In our world full of strangers, estranged from their own past, culture and country, from their neighbors, friends and family, from their deepest self and their God, we witness a painful search for a hospitable place where life can be lived without fear and where community can be found."[3]

The very estrangement that Nouwen describes could be understood to be the source of so much fear. Other religious traditions emphasize this as well. The Upanishads, ancient Indian scriptures, suggest that the source of fear is duality: "Assuredly, it is from experiencing a second entity that fear arises."[4] This scripture suggests that when we understand the world as being made up of "me" and "not me," of "self" and "other," fear arises. The "ego," in the sense of focusing on "me" or "I," becomes like a wall built between us and others. Our emotions, if unnoticed, become like bricks in that wall. Unrecognized feelings like fear and anger can easily reinforce the separation between "us" and "them" as we try to "protect" our ego-selves.

Applying our awareness practices, however, can begin to break down this wall of separation between self and other, and open up new worlds, new awareness, new possibilities for hospitality. The practices can change the fortress of the heart into the garden of the heart. Buddhist teacher Henepola Gunaratana puts it this way: "Thus, as genuine mindfulness is built up, the walls of the ego itself are broken down, craving diminishes, defensiveness and rigidity lessen, you become more open, accepting, and flexible. You learn to share your loving kindness."[5] That sounds like receptivity, reverence, and generosity to me.

Swami Anantananda, in his book *What's On My Mind?* describes fear as an *e-motion*, reminding us that fear, like other emotions, moves through us rather than lives in us.[6] It only becomes a permanent resident inside us if we try to avoid or repress it. When we become afraid of our fear, we can become paralyzed by it, and it gets stuck inside us. On the other hand, when we can witness our fear with awareness, it takes on its natural quality of motion and fluidity. It arises and passes away naturally if we can allow it to do so.

Letting fear course through our body will allow us to tap into the energy that fear contains. For example, while I was writing this chapter, a spider dropped from the ceiling and dangled by its invisible thread about eight inches from my face. When I saw it, I leapt out of my chair filled with energy (to say the least). That is fear as an e-motion, which Swami Anantananda describes as "a motion of energy outward."[7] This is one of the positive elements of fear. Another is fear as excitement. Sometimes when we are afraid, we experience that fear as a thrill; Anantananda likens it to going on a roller coaster or riding a horse fast. Remembering a moment like this in your own life, when you experienced fear as excitement, can help you accept your fear and use its power for transformation, rather than stagnation, on your journey to hospitality.

ENCOUNTERING GOD IN OUR FEAR

The ancient Indian scripture the *Taittiriya Upanishad* speaks about fear in relation to Brahman. Brahman is the Sanskrit word for the ultimate reality and ground of the universe[8]—what I would refer to in English as God. The Upanishad says, "To the man who thinks himself learned and yet knows himself not as

Brahman—Brahman, who drives away all fear, appears as fear itself." In other words, if we see our mystical identity with God—the ground of the universe—we will have no fear, because ultimate reality drives away all fear. But if we feel separate from that ultimate reality, then that God, that ground of the universe, will appear in our life as fear itself. Separation creates the fear.

Swami Anantananda does something fascinating with this scripture. "What if," he suggests, "we recognized or remembered that our fear is a form of God's energy within us? What if we remembered that when we stop fighting off this energy called fear, we stop fighting off God? Then God is there with us as an *ally* in the situation—not only as an ally, but as our own energy!"[9] When we embrace fear as a kind of holy energy, our own energy but also the energy of God, this emotion becomes *motion*; it can be a source of power, enabling us to move through whatever situation we are facing. The key is that we let fear exist without repressing or denying it. We actually embrace it as a transformative life energy rather than get paralyzed by it. We can move through it, and it can move through us. This is practicing receptivity and reverence toward our fear—inviting and welcoming it as it is.

Escorting Yourself through Moments of Fear

Everybody's fear is different, so you will have to be in charge of identifying how it lives and works in you. One thing I notice is that some people respond to fear by getting quiet and withholding the self, and some respond by getting very loud and pushing the self toward others. This can be very subtle or very dramatic. Even talking excessively can be a way to cover up your fear. Look deep inside yourself for your fear; look in places you might not expect to find it. Maybe you can sit down with a piece of paper and pen and ask yourself, "What am I afraid of? What am I afraid of?" Make a list. The next day, make another list.

Once you have identified a fear, here are some steps you can take to practice escorting yourself through fear so you can step into your courage and rediscover the receptivity, reverence, and generosity that will enable you to move from estrangement to kinship through hospitality.

Acknowledge your fear. When you notice that you feel fear or anxiety, acknowledge it by naming it. Say to yourself something like "I feel afraid." This is basic awareness practice, and naming it is the first step of acceptance. Here it is, right now, inside me.

Explore your fear. Once you notice it, consider where in your body you feel fear. Is it a sensation in your stomach, queasiness perhaps? Do you clutch it in your shoulders and tense your back? How is your breathing affected by fear? Does it become more shallow? Are your breaths quick and short? Or does the tightness in your abdomen prevent you from getting the air that you really need to function well? Our bodies respond differently, so it's an important part of awareness practice to see how emotions move through or get stuck in your own body.

Embrace your fear. Rather than hiding your fear or denying it, embrace it. After noticing its physical location in your body, imagine the fear expanding and filling your whole body. Imagine it washing over you like a shower, or let it course through your body as though it were electricity. It might feel something like shivering.

This might be a helpful analogy. When we walk in the cold, we tend to tense up our bodies in an effort to keep the cold out. We scrunch up our shoulders and contract everything we can in hope that the cold won't get *into* us. It's counterintuitive to relax our body and open our posture when we're in the cold. But when we do, our body naturally shivers and warms us up. The cold dissipates and warmth permeates us.

The same is true of fear. When we are afraid of letting the fear enter us or run through our bodies, we tend to brace ourselves against it, deny it, or suppress it. Opening to it is like opening to the cold air. Let it course through you like a shiver, like electricity making the hair on your arms stand on end. When we do this, it quickly passes through us and fades away.

Allow fear to dissipate. You can practice embracing your fear when it comes up in your daily life. Practice in advance so that you're more likely to remember it when the fear confronts you. One way to practice is to stand in a dark room at night—turn off all the lights and stand in the dark. There in the dark you have a blank slate for your imagination. Imagine things that frighten you, and notice the onset of fear. Notice where it goes in your body, and let it go there! Notice what fear literally feels like in your body. The moment you feel the fear, turn your attention to this process of fear moving through you. Don't focus on the content of what you are afraid of. Instead, focus on the energy the fear brings into you. Each time the fear rises up in you, let it course through you one more time. When you allow yourself to experience your fear, you can become less afraid of the emotion itself.

Finally, try introducing new names for your experience of fear. See how your experience changes when you call your fear *excitement*, as Swami Anantananda suggests. Can you tap into the experience of that by making a mental shift? Try remembering that this e-motion is the very energy of God, the power of the Life of life, the presence of ultimate reality coursing through you. Whatever it is, see the holy in it. Does naming it the energy of God change your experience of fear?

By practicing these steps, not only are you escorting yourself through the experience of fear, but God is also escorting you through it.

When you change your understanding of fear, you can find holy power inside it. You find that you are not alone, not separate. In fact, divinity is fully present with you, even in your fear. This is a powerful antidote to estrangement—when you begin to lessen the gap between you and God, in a mystical sense. When you do, you also chip away at the estrangement between yourself and others.

Once you do this exercise a few times, you will realize that fear is a lot less dangerous than you might think. Often it is our fear of fear that paralyzes us. Practicing and remembering that fear rises and passes away like every other thought or emotion can be liberating, because fear then ceases to have the power to control or debilitate us.

Fear works against hospitality because when we allow fear to solidify in us, it becomes a wall we can hide behind to prevent others from seeing us for who we are. At other times, fear can cause us to look away from other people: We meet a homeless person on the street and we're afraid of the magnitude of his hunger and his need. We meet a person who doesn't speak our language and we're afraid of our inability to communicate— afraid that we or she will be embarrassed or frustrated. We meet a person of any people-group different from our own—different race, class, religion, gender, sexual orientation, nationality, or ability—about whom we have been taught stereotypes and we are afraid the stereotypes might be true. Or we are afraid that the person we're meeting might think that we think the stereotypes are true. Fear is abundant, and unless we can make friends with our fear it will continue to control us and diminish our capacities to be receptive, reverent, and generous. We will continue to live in the illusion of separation, a stranger in a world of strangers, never really connecting, heart to heart. But we don't have to be controlled by fear in any of these ways. We can embrace our fear and acknowledge our vulnerability in order to become more free. Rather than let our fears cause us to close down, we can open up and encounter others in the spaciousness of the heart.

DISTINGUISHING APPROPRIATE BOUNDARIES: TRUSTING YOUR INTUITION

The prior exercise has to do with understanding our fear itself. If we do that practice, it can help us when we encounter fearful situations in person, especially when fear is based on false perceptions and projections. At other times, however, fear is warranted and can give us the energy to protect ourselves. Whether our fear is stimulated by real danger or false perceptions, becoming familiar with our fear will help us remain active, responsive, and empowered. Rather than preventing us from being hospitable by causing us to freeze up, fear becomes just one more human e-motion that courses through our lives and helps us grow into more receptive, reverent, and generous people.

The following exercise is about assessing fear as it relates to our physical safety. In situations of potential physical danger it is important to trust our intuition. But to do that, we have to practice realizing what our intuition is, as well as where our fear comes from.

Trusting your intuition means looking deeply into a situation. Awareness and perception are central. Pay attention to the people you feel cautious about. If you get a bad feeling in the pit of your stomach because of something someone says to you, or the way she touches you or approaches you, don't look away, either metaphorically or literally. Acknowledge that feeling and look more deeply into it. Don't say, "It's probably nothing." Ask yourself, "What *is* it?"

Intuition lies deeper in us than fear does, so we have to reach through the fear and into perception. We can look for our intuition by examining the sensations in our own bodies. What is that feeling of tightness in your shoulders, or that uneasiness in your stomach? Do you recognize it from other experiences? What is triggering these reactions?

Remember, God is present, even in fear. If there is fear, remember that the energy of God, the Life of our life, is present in this fear. By accepting and allowing the fear, we also accept the energy that the fear generates in us. Take God's hand in this fear and allow that presence to escort you through, or out of, the situation.

Allow yourself to assess the situation step by step. Don't force yourself to trust someone that you don't trust. Trust step by step. Express a small degree of openness and see what happens. If it feels in your intuition that you are safe, open just a step more. If not, pull back. It's okay to leave a situation that feels unsafe or harmful in any way. Or, depending on the circumstances, it might be better to firmly ask the other person to leave.

Sometimes you just can't tell where your fears are coming from. Maybe you're projecting your assumptions onto other people or onto situations that you *expect* to be fearful. Or maybe you're intuiting a very real danger. Sometimes it can be difficult to tell the difference, which is why the step-by-step method of discernment is helpful. But even with that, sometimes we just don't know. Then we discern how much risk we are willing to take.

People have been discussing and debating issues of keeping appropriate boundaries in hospitality throughout recorded history. So don't feel bad that you have to think about it today, too. You just have to be aware of how you think about it. Reformation theologian John Calvin wrote, "Let us beware that we seek not cover for our stinginess under the shadow of prudence."[10] In other words, sometimes "playing it safe" can be an excuse for a lack of generosity. Stinginess can mean stinginess of heart as well as stinginess of hand. Calvin is encouraging us to push ourselves a little further than we might think we are able to go to take a risk for the sake of generosity and relationship.

Sometimes this kind of risk is very important in hospitality. It can be a great gift to give someone, to give ourselves, to reach through fear and beyond the barriers that separate us. Precious human contact can make a huge impact in changing someone's life, our own included. Taking risks stretches us and helps us grow. Risky hospitality sometimes bears great fruit. Martha Nussbaum, reflecting on the *Fragility of Goodness*, says that "there is a beauty in the willingness to love someone in the face of love's instability and worldliness," a beauty that is not present in the same way in a "completely trustworthy love."[11] Sometimes taking a risk for love, or for the hospitality extended through loving actions, makes the value of the hospitality so much greater. Discerning which boundaries are appropriate boundaries and which boundaries are detrimental is one of the most difficult tasks in hospitality.

PURSUING KINSHIP RATHER THAN ESTRANGEMENT

There is a basic human sensation of separation and "otherness" that is important to be aware of as we consider our practices of hospitality. When we see people as strangers, we have a choice about whether we will see them as fundamentally different from us or as intrinsically similar. It's a question of how we understand the differences between us. Dwelling on the distinctions between us can concretize or harden them. This thought process reinforces our belief in our identity as "different" and others as "strangers."

Comparing ourselves to others by emphasizing the contrasts always leads to the same state, says Buddhist teacher Henepola Gunaratana—"estrangement, barriers between people, and ill feeling."[12] Gunaratana's teaching on this provides a great resource for practice as we consider hospitality to strangers, because these practices can give us insight into our tendencies to reinforce estrangement by our thoughts and the actions that naturally flow from these thoughts.

Gunaratana describes inner "hindrances" that prevent us from seeing things the way they truly are and from resting in our

Buddha nature. Buddha nature is our ultimate essence, which Gunaratana describes as "pure, holy, and inherently good."[13] When we are able to rest in this nature, we experience ourselves as fully alive, taking nothing for granted, experiencing everything with vitality as a living, changing process. As a Christian, I correlate this idea of Buddha nature with my understanding of the image of God at the core of every human being. It's that "pure, holy, and inherently good" quality that is somehow intrinsically present in us, but which we often do not fully realize or embody in our lives.

The hindrances, such as greed, lust, hatred, and aversion, keep us from resting in that pure, holy, inherently good nature that is somehow our ultimate essence. Fear is another hindrance. Gunaratana also calls these hindrances "defilements," because they cloud the purity of our Buddha nature. All of these hindrances reinforce our belief that we are inherently separate from others. "Greed and lust are attempts to get 'some of that' for me; hatred and aversion are attempts to place greater distance between 'me and that.' All the defilements depend upon the perception of a barrier between self and other, and all of them foster this perception every time they are exercised."[14]

Rather than focus on the distinctions between people, Gunaratana suggests that it is better to replace this unskillful state of mind with a more skillful one. Through awareness practices, we can center our attention on things that are universal human experiences; this will bring us closer to others, rather than pushing us apart. This kind of comparison "leads to feelings of kinship rather than feelings of estrangement."[15]

The universal human experiences that Gunaratana suggests we look for, and that can lead to feelings of kinship, are the internal processes that have to do with how we think and how we react to things. When we encounter something (a person or a thought or an object—it doesn't matter), a reaction rises up in us. It can be a positive, negative, or neutral response. It can be a feeling—anger, pride, fear, affection, fascination. It can be a memory of the past or a fantasy of the future. Though the contents may differ from person to person or culture to culture, the process itself is the same; when we encounter something, a reaction rises up in us.

Becoming aware of this process, and seeing that it is a fundamentally human process, leads us to an acceptance of ourselves and others. There is a kind of forgiveness inherent in this kind of acceptance. We let go of judging because we see that this is how people are, ourselves included. When feelings of anger come up in us, we can say to ourselves, "Oh, I'm having this very human experience of anger. This is what people do." Becoming *aware* and *accepting* it at this level can then lead to us being more responsible about *how we express* our anger (or any emotion)— *awareness, acceptance, action*—our old triadic friend. Accepting that our experience is human doesn't mean giving permission for acting out. Instead, it creates space for forgiveness and compassion, which in turn creates the opportunity for us to respond to our feelings rather than react. In other words, we become more free and able to choose how we will act.

Becoming aware of these human processes and tendencies will help us grow in hospitality. Gunaratana describes some of these beneficial transformations: "We become very understanding people as a result. We no longer get upset by the 'failings' of others. We progress toward harmony with all life."[16] This kind of understanding will enable us to see past our illusions of estrangement, and to extend welcome and hospitality in reverent, generous ways, human to human, bozo to bozo, bus-mate to bus-mate. On this fundamental level, no one is a stranger. We are all on this bus together.

PRIDEFULNESS AND SHAME: TWO SIDES OF THE SAME EGO

Besides fear, pridefulness and shame are also significant obstacles to practicing hospitality toward strangers. Pridefulness is an arrogant kind of pride, as opposed to a healthier kind of pride that is based on a reverent respect of the self. Pridefulness is often exhibited by those who have inflated egos, who are self-absorbed and generally don't care about, or even "look down" on, others. Pridefulness gets in the way of hospitality because it, and the ego underneath it, is fundamentally based on duality—the comparative distinctions between self/other, as well as judgments of good/bad, better/worse. It boils down to the dualistic ideas "I am better" or "I am worse" than others. All of us experience this to some degree. While pridefulness is comparative—it's a kind of judgment—self-respect is based on the inherent value of the self and is not comparative. It's a kind of love and honor, based in respect for our Buddha nature, "pure, holy, and inherently good."

If pridefulness means believing in the duality that, compared to "others," *I* am "better," then shame is just the flip side. Shame often results when you believe that, compared to "others," *I* am "worse." With this understanding we can say that shame is an egotistical feeling, because it is centered (perhaps obsessively so) on the self. Pridefulness and shame both make it very difficult to extend open-hearted hospitality to others, because while we are stuck in judging our own value (better/worse), we are also stuck judging the value of others (better/worse). This is the comparative thinking that reinforces estrangement, barriers between people, and ill will.

Pridefulness prevents us from being truly receptive of the beauty and inherent value of others, because we aren't able to welcome them reverently if we believe that they are less than us. There is no generosity stemming from pride, only patronage. Similarly, shame prevents us from extending hospitality, because in judging ourselves as less than, our own hearts become atrophied. The garden of our heart becomes filled with shadows and humiliation, and we think there is no living garden inside us in which to welcome others.

If we can notice that we feel pridefulness or that we feel shame, then we are well on our way to hospitality, because with noticing, things begin to change. Noticing pridefulness or shame, we can remember, "Ah, this is ego." We can decide to be gentle with ourselves, and take this opportunity to see, not how we are different from others, but how we are the same.

However, looking for spiritual unity doesn't require us to deny the obvious diversity that exists in the world; it simply invites us to put it into perspective. Diversity is worth celebrating, as Swami Anantananda reminds us: "Comparative differences per se are not only *not* the problem, they make play! Hooray, in fact, for differences. But do we see it as play? Where is our identity centered? Do we remember our shared divinity regardless of our role or position in the play? Or do we forget and live as if the differences are who we really are?"[17] Anantananda's comment reminds us to ask, "Who am I, really?" Answering this question by remembering our shared humanity with all people can lead us from estrangement to kinship, with each person manifesting the secret beauty of his or her heart in a unique way.

COMPASSION MEANS BEING WITH

There is a kind of deep with-ness available to us as human beings if we can only realize and embrace it. This with-ness turns estrangement into playful diversity, a spiritual intimacy that we share even with "strangers" through our interbeing. We can deny this connection at any time, but we can also turn toward it and prepare ourselves to perceive it and live into its truth.

I'm talking about compassion, a quality that is inherent in our Buddha nature and one that we can practice uncovering within ourselves. The word literally means to "suffer with," but it's not primarily about suffering. Compassion is primarily about love, and the "with" is a very important part of compassion.

Buddhist teacher Cheri Huber says that "compassion is an experience of respect, of admiration, of appreciation. When someone is going through a difficult or painful time and we admire their courage, respect their journey, and offer support—that is compassion. Compassion doesn't assume there's something wrong that needs to be fixed or changed."[18] Instead, when we are compassionate we are simply present with our fellow humans as they are, without trying to change them. At the same time, if we are fully present with someone who is suffering because of injustice, we are more likely to become committed to correcting the injustice if we are truly present with the individuals who are suffering. We also become able to more accurately perceive the source of the problem if we don't look away from the actual experiences of others.

Being engaged like this is a very hospitable way to express compassion, because it implies a deep receptivity, an openness to the experience of others, along with a deep reverence of their inherent value. The generosity offered in this kind of compassion is the generosity of presence, full attention that does not create estrangement or separation. When we are really being *with* someone in compassion, Huber suggests that "for a brief moment, at a level most of us are unaware of, there is an experience that the 'other' is not other. For just a flash, in a timeless, spaceless nonplace, we are one; we are not separate. A child falls down, a friend is disappointed, and we intuitively sense their goodness, their innocence, and their inherent purity. We feel that same goodness; we *are* that goodness. Our heart opens to that other being. That is compassion."[19]

As we learn to open our hearts and set aside our attachments to ego and estrangement, we will continue to grow more skillful at holding the shared humanity of each other in a safe and gentle space between us, not making assumptions about each other, but always curious to learn more about each individual we encounter. Through this deeper knowing of each other, we're sure to learn more about differences in culture and gender and sexuality and age and ability and religious experience. But more than that, we'll be learning to accept and revere the mystery and diversity of creation.

THE PARABLE OF THE LONG-HANDLED SPOONS: GENEROSITY AND MUTUALITY

Estrangement is a mind-set that we can cling to or set aside. We can reinforce or undermine systems of estrangement by our decisions about how to interact with our fellow human beings. This is illustrated well in the following fable.

> Once there was a seeker who desired to see what heaven and hell were like. In answer to her prayers, she was miraculously transported to the doorway of hell. Pushing it open hesitantly, she looked in to see a cold stone room with a small fire in the center, over which simmered a pot of soup. The smell was wonderful. This soup made her mouth water and her stomach growl immediately. She was surprised, however, to see people everywhere looking emaciated and moaning. As she watched for a while, she realized that everyone was carrying a spoon with an enormously long handle, longer than their arms. They repeatedly approached the simmering stew, took out a spoonful, and inevitably spilled it as they tried to turn the spoon into their mouth. No one was able to eat at all! She shuddered and slammed the door quickly.
>
> Immediately, she found herself in front of another door. "This must be heaven," she thought. Again, she pushed open the door slowly and gazed in. The very same scene greeted her eyes—cold stone room, small fire, simmering soup. But here the people seemed different. They were smiling and talking with each other. They seemed well fed and healthy. She studied the scene and saw that

they did indeed have the same ridiculously long-handled spoons. As she continued to watch, she saw the people feeding each other, reaching the long-handled spoons in every direction throughout the room. The mouth-watering soup actually nourished and warmed them because they gave it to each other.[20]

In this story, the people in "heaven" had overcome their estrangement from one another, replacing it with hospitality. They acknowledged their own and one another's vulnerabilities and incapacities—they were hungry and they couldn't feed themselves. They encountered that vulnerability with mutuality and respect, realizing that they didn't have to stay isolated and focused on themselves. Instead of isolation in their hunger, they chose to embody deep with-ness. Com (with)-passion.

With this kind of shift, we suddenly change the entire dynamic and begin creating a system in which people are fed. And since we are part of the system, we find that we are fed, too. This is the essence of mutuality, which is based on generosity. We give, we serve, and somehow, mysteriously, we find that we receive—not because we demand or expect it, but simply because that is the nature of receptive, reverent generosity. That is what hospitality looks like in community. With-ness happens. Compassion happens.

Ana María Pineda, in *Practicing Our Faith*, explains that "the word that means 'stranger' in Greek [*xenos*], also means 'guest' and 'host.'" In the New Testament, hospitality is *philoxenia*, love of the stranger/guest/host. It is a circular relationship in which no one is truly a stranger and yet we are all, somehow, strangers, guests *and* hosts. Pineda writes, "This one word [*xenos*] signals the essential mutuality that is at the heart of hospitality. No one is strange except in relation to someone else; we make one another guests and hosts by how we treat one another."[21] In *philoxenia*, estrangement disappears, because we welcome the

Buddha nature, the inherent goodness that is present in those we encounter.

PUTTING GENEROSITY INTO ACTION

It isn't always easy to put this philosophical ideal into practice. But there is hope in the fact that we can learn from each other and we can change, first simply by paying attention and noticing what we haven't noticed before. As Nouwen points out, "When we are willing to detach ourselves from making our own limited experience the criterion for our approach to others, we may be able to see that life is greater than our life, history is greater than our history, experience greater than our experience and God greater than our God. That is the poverty of heart that makes a good host."[22] This kind of "poverty" refers to the spaciousness of a heart that is uncluttered and open to new experience and understanding.

When learning to put hospitality into action, it's okay to begin with small steps, even missteps. One day I was walking home from a wonderful Caribbean restaurant with a friend. We were each carrying square white take-out packages with our leftovers. I had been talking with my friend in the restaurant about how wonderful these leftovers would be for my next meal. As we left the restaurant, a man came up to us on the street, asking for money. I felt very nervous, as I often have when approached on the street, wondering whether this person would let me go by peacefully or become confrontational. We said we couldn't give him any money and I started to walk away. But my friend said to him, "Would you like some food?" His eyes lit up and he said emphatically, "Yes." She gave him her take-out box.

Then they both turned and looked at me. I looked down at my take-out box and thought about the delicious food in there. It was from my favorite restaurant. I hesitated. I was unprepared to let it go. My friend saw the hesitation in my face and turned to the man and said, "Enjoy that. God bless you." She was gracefully taking the attention off of me and she began to walk on. I joined her with a guilty pang in my heart. I admired the openness and the gracious giving that she had shown to the man and to me. I don't know what she was feeling inside, but I only experienced her grace and compassion.

This was compassion in the sense that she didn't try to change me and didn't seem to judge me. She just saw me and saw my unfinished, imperfect human state. But she also saw the man, the "stranger" we encountered, and she greeted him with an open heart, a compassionate heart that seemed to make no assumptions but was simply present with him in that moment. She simply offered what she had. I had never seen this kind of respectful love in action in quite that way, and I was changed by seeing her receptive, reverent heart. I saw her awareness that she is connected to the unknown man on the street—in fact, I saw that he was known because she looked at him with "knowing" eyes, eyes willing to take him in, see him deeply, and greet the holiness in him.

Shortly after that experience, I went again to that same restaurant with another friend. On that day we had eaten lightly so as to save room for key lime pie in honor of my friend's birthday. When we left, we left with two take-out boxes, and you can guess what's coming next. The universe has its own way of offering second chances and opportunities for us to grow and change. A different man came up to us, asking for money. We told him we had no money to give him but I remembered my earlier experience and blurted out, "Would you like some food?" His eyes lit up and he said emphatically, "Yes." It was as though I was in the cold stone room with a long-handled spoon, and I had finally taken the leap to turn it away from my own mouth and extend it toward someone else. This changed me. It changed my heart. I opened the gates of the moat protecting my heart, and the water rushed out into the castle garden, a living garden in which to meet people.

On a fundamental level I realized that I am in relationship with this man—not estranged. The dissolution of estrangement, the way it fades away when we look past it, doesn't mean that we will be friends with every person we meet. I may never see that particular man again. But I know that I am in relationship with him, and in some way, whatever I do with my life will affect him. It brings to mind the poetic expression of this idea written by Martin Luther King Jr. in his Letter from Birmingham Jail: "We are caught in an inescapable network of mutuality, tied in a single garment of destiny. Whatever affects one directly, affects all indirectly."[23] Love, compassion, with-ness—these all break down the illusions of estrangement and bring us back to our own center, where we encounter God and beloved self together, dwelling in the hub of all sacred spaces, a heart broken open wide enough to encounter with reverence and generosity other hearts, other children of God.

HOSPITALITY TO ENEMIES

Extending Generosity through Non-Retaliation

Mike was six years old in 1935, and living in Atlanta, Georgia, where he had been friends with his white playmate since they were three years old. Mike was African-American, and his friend's father owned a shop across the street from Mike's house, where they played almost every day. When they turned six, they started going to school, in separate schools of course, because this was the time of segregation and Jim Crow laws.

One day, Mike was shocked when his friend told him that his father wouldn't let him play with Mike anymore. Mike went home to his parents and asked why this would be. At the dinner table that night they discussed it, his parents telling him about racism for the first time in his life. They described the tragedy of it all, and told Mike about some of the personal insults they had suffered. At six years old, he says, he became determined to hate every white person. Though his parents told him that it was his Christian duty to love all people, he asked himself, "How could I love a race of people who hated me and who had been responsible for breaking me up with one of my best childhood friends?"[1]

That is the question before us in this chapter: How can we love in the face of hatred? How can we prepare ourselves for and then implement hospitality in the presence of hostility? How is it possible to hold *receptivity*, *reverence*, and *generosity* toward those who hold enmity toward us?

Hostility isn't always as obvious as that found in racism such as Mike experienced. Enmity happens at all levels of intensity, from the cold shoulder to the angry stare to brutal violence. Preparing to respond to such hostility begins from our center, the place inside ourself where we have personal power. We touched upon this idea in chapter 4, when we considered the possibility of shifting our focus from our vulnerability in the face of others to instead realizing our own power to act as proactive neighbors in all our encounters. This describes an embrace of self-aware personal power that is also essential in our efforts to embody hospitality in our encounters with enemies and hostility of all sorts.

The inward preparations that we make will help us in all our outward encounters. The secret is in learning to focus on what is happening and how we are responding *here* and *now*, which in turn enables us to tap into our center of personal power. *Here and now* is the place in which we are powerful. Here and now is the place where hospitality and love begin to change everything, not because *we* are changing everything, but because love changes everything.

Some types of hostility seem too big and too systemic for us to imagine overcoming them with hospitality or love. With Mike, we have to wonder how we could possibly love someone who hates us. It surely isn't easy; sometimes it feels impossible. But breaking out of the stranglehold of hostility and hatred is the only way that we will ever be spiritually free.

We have a lot to learn from Mike. As he grew up and matured, he became a leader who we still revere today. He learned for himself and then led many to embrace love as the only antidote for hate. He took on his father's first name, Martin, and today we know him as The Reverend Doctor Martin Luther King Jr.

SOUL FORCE

In 1931, four years before Martin's (or Mike's) formative childhood experience in Atlanta, *Time* magazine ran a story under the headline, "Soul Force."[2] They put it in quotes, just like that, because it was a new phrase, one that many people may not have recognized. It was a term coined by Mohandas K. Gandhi, and the spiritual practice it represents has changed millions of lives.

Soul force is *satyagraha*, holding on to Truth (*satya*). It's the word that Gandhi chose to describe the particular form of active nonviolence that he brought to India. He equated Truth with the soul, the power of love that upholds the entire universe. "Truth is my God,"[3] he said, and he meant that this force of truth/love/soul *was* God. "I do dimly perceive that whilst everything around me is ever changing, ever dying, there is underlying all that change a Living Power that is changeless, that holds all together, that creates, dissolves, and recreates. That informing Power or Spirit is God. And since nothing else I see merely through the senses can or will persist, He alone is."[4]

Drawing close to this Truth means realizing the power and presence of God within us and acting out of that awareness. In the here and now of Gandhi's life he came face-to-face with violence and enmity. He was challenged to put his deep theological ideals into action in a way that would make love real in situations where it seemed there was no place for love. Gandhi's insight was that there was strength in love and power in nonviolence. He did not teach *passive* resistance to injustice but *active* nonviolence toward adversaries, and non-cooperation with systems that create harm.

The power of love and truth that enables Soul Force is a power relevant to all our relationships. Gandhi described it this way, saying, "Thousands, indeed tens of thousands, depend for their existence on a very active working of this force. Little quarrels of millions of families in their daily lives disappear before the exercise of this force."[5] *Satyagraha*, or holding on to this truth and love with firmness, is a method of working for the common good of the world, and yet it begins inside us and can change how we act in all our relationships. It is the power that makes deep, spiritually transformative hospitality possible in the face of hostility.

CLAIMING OUR PERSONAL POWER

Gandhi is credited with bringing about the independence of India from British colonial rule in 1947 because of the way he led masses of people, through his teachings and his example, to resist unjust treatment. People called him "Mahatma" or Great Soul (*maha atma*), and by 1931 they were calling him a saint. But this is what he said of himself: "You must not think me supernatural. I am only a *satyagrahi* [one who practices truth force, love force, soul force]. I am but a humble servant. I am only common clay."[6] *Time* magazine reports that he said this "gravely" to the "clamoring worshipping populace." Gandhi's grave tone indicates to us how very important this point is. He saw how detrimental and dangerous it is when people forfeit their own greatness by giving it to others—they rob themselves of their own power.

Martin Luther King Jr. made a similar point when he said of himself at a mass meeting in the middle of the Montgomery bus boycott in 1956, "I want you to know that if M. L. King had never been born this movement would have taken place. I just happened to be here. You know there comes a time when time itself is ready for change. That time has come in Montgomery, and I had nothing to do with it."[7] Dr. King, like Mahatma Gandhi, lived and acted and loved in the here and now of his time. And we can do that, too.

The minute we begin to put the people we admire up on a pedestal is the minute we begin to dehumanize them and disempower ourselves. Dr. King was incredible precisely because he sat at the kitchen table in the middle of the night, afraid, and prayed to God for courage because he knew he was too weak to face the violence and the hatred that his stand for justice drew to him.[8] Gandhi inspired millions because he took his spiritual practice of *satygraha* seriously.

Dr. King said, "I just happened to be here." And Gandhi said, "I am only common clay." They are both telling us—I'm just a person, just like you, doing the best I can, doing my spiritual practices. Our place of power is inside us, rooted and grounded in the here and now of a living power that is love, firmness, and non-violence. This is the Truth of *satyagraha*, soul force, and it can shape us into people of hospitality based in receptivity, reverence, and generosity, even in the most trying of circumstances.

LOVE WINS

Just nineteen months after *Time* published the article titled "Soul Force," it published a follow-up article titled *Soul Force Wins*.[9] They didn't have to put it in quotes, because by then so many people had heard of it. Looking for and holding to that love and Truth was what gave Gandhi and his followers the power to pursue justice by actively embracing their adversaries with love.

Years after Gandhi's teaching empowered a nation and led India to independence from British rule, Martin Luther King Jr. had begun to talk about similar beliefs and methods in Montgomery, Alabama. "Christ furnished the spirit and motivation," Dr. King said, "while Gandhi furnished the method."[10] A year after the Montgomery bus boycott ended, nearly two years after his home was bombed, and twenty-two years after his childhood friend rejected him because of his race, Dr. King preached a sermon at Dexter Avenue Baptist Church in Montgomery called "Loving Your Enemies."[11]

Although King does not use the language of "hospitality" in this sermon, his insight into the challenges of loving our enemies shines a direct light on what it takes to practice hospitality in the face of hostility. Dr. King's sermon takes as its starting point a well-known verse in the New Testament in which Jesus teaches, "You have heard that it was said, 'You shall love your neighbor and hate your enemy.' But I say to you, Love your enemies and pray for those who persecute you, so that you may be children of your Father in heaven; for he makes his sun rise on the evil and on the good, and sends rain on the righteous and on the unrighteous."[12]

But how can we possibly love those who hate us? In the sermon, Dr. King gives three suggestions about how to love our enemies. First, he says, we must examine ourselves for our possible contributions to the enmity; second, we must try to see the good in our enemies and remember the evil that is in us; and third, we must resist the temptation to defeat our enemies.[13]

These three actions resonate with our paradigm of hospitality based on the movements of in-with-out. *Receptivity* has to do with our inner state of full awareness, which allows us to see ourselves and others accurately, and parallels Dr. King's encouragement that we examine ourselves. *Reverence* describes the nature of our attitude toward others and our act of remembering our shared humanity, seeing the divinity, or image of God, within everyone— much as does King's emphasis on finding both the good and the evil in ourselves and our adversaries. And finally, *generosity* suggests that we carefully and thoughtfully choose our actions toward others—which correlates with Dr. King's urging that we not defeat our enemies, even when we have the opportunity to do so.

Even though Dr. King sought to defeat injustice and the evils of segregation and racism, he taught that this is different from defeating people. In reaction to oppression, Dr. King said that we have three choices of how to respond. We can resist oppression with physical violence, which Dr. King saw as ultimately futile; we can acquiesce and give in to oppression with resignation; or we can build large-scale, organized resistance to oppression using only the tools of nonviolence and love.[14]

Both Dr. King and Mahatma Gandhi worked in the realm of social change and took their ideas beyond individual and personal practice into the practices of communities and countries. Gandhi said, "We have to make truth and non-violence not matters for mere individual practice but for practice by groups and communities and nations."[15] But both leaders taught that the foundation of such social movement is rooted in individual practice. Individual integrity empowers community transformation.

In his sermon about loving our enemies, Dr. King essentially taught how we can prepare ourselves to make a real difference in the world, both personally and socially. Without calling it "soul force" in this sermon, he talked about tapping into that transformative power of love that Gandhi also believed in. Dr. King called it the "redemptive power" of love, and said that this power of love is the only force that can ultimately transform individuals and our world.[16]

So let's look at the three foundational steps that Dr. King suggested for loving—or practicing hospitality toward—our enemies.

WHY DO THEY HATE US?

When considering love, Dr. King encouraged his listeners, and us, to examine ourselves first, because there might be something that we are doing, either on a subtle level or in an explicit way, to stimulate what King called "the tragic hate response." [17] If so, then the only way we'll be able to address and adjust that is by becoming aware of it. It requires us to be relentlessly honest in our self-examination. This is the basic first step of hospitality.

Sometimes when people seem to hate us, it makes no sense. We can't see the reason why. We can't think of anything we have done that would elicit such a reaction. Once I had a job working in an office that was shared by three people, and our work areas were divided into cubicles by free-standing dividers. This meant that we had no privacy, that our phone calls, though we spoke softly, might be overheard by others.

During my first week of work, I heard one of my coworkers refer to me on the phone as "the new chick" and call me "that b—," a very derogatory term, her voice dripping with hostility. I was shocked. I hadn't done anything or said anything mean or hateful. I felt horribly and unfairly judged and somewhat paralyzed by the venomous attitude she began to project onto me. Why would she hate me like this?

At the time it felt so completely unfair. It seemed I had been only kind and open to her. But looking back on it now, I wonder, did I start to dislike her only after she called me awful names to her friends on the phone, or did I dislike her before she started doing that? She was a bit unkempt and somewhat edgy, seeming to spend a lot of her work time surfing the Internet and being sarcastic and irritable. Did I have a subtle judgmental attitude toward her that she sensed and responded to by shutting me out of her inner circle? Was she trying to protect herself against being criticized by criticizing me first? Was she trying to drown out my subtle judgmental "vibe" by criticizing me more loudly or more directly than I was judging her? Maybe there was something in me that had aroused the tragic hate response in her.

Sometimes, though, people hate or dislike us not because of anything that we have done, but because of human tendencies toward jealously, greed, fear, and shame. Could my office mate have hated me because she was insecure and hated herself? Because I reminded her of someone who had treated her badly in the past? Because she felt jealous, fearful, or ashamed? I would never know. In the meantime, what would be an effective response? At the time, I tended to internalize her negativity toward me, feeling bad about myself because she didn't seem to like me. I had enough self-awareness to *try* not to do that, but it is a difficult spiritual practice. I knew that to become angry toward her, adding my own hateful or disdainful attitude to her hostility, would only exacerbate the problem. I was able to act without hostility, but I don't think I achieved generosity. I worked on receptivity and reverence, in the sense of looking for the good in her and looking for the good in me, too, so as not to act hostile toward myself. It was only later that I tried looking for the part of me that might have somehow triggered some of her hostility toward me.

This kind of self-aware examination is something that Dr. King recommended not only at the individual level, but also at the community level and at the level of international relations. The burning issues in his day were different from ours in the particulars, but perhaps similar to ours in the human dimensions. Then, society was facing an ideological struggle between Communism and democracy, embodied in the Cold War between the United States and the Soviet Union.

Now we face other ideological struggles. To be honest in our engagement with these issues and problems, to try to answer the question of "why do they hate us," we need to consider the possibility that we have done something "deep down in our past," as Dr. King said, that has on some level provoked a response of hatred and hostility. If we can't acknowledge what we have done, we deprive ourselves of the opportunity to grow as people and as a culture. We deny ourselves the opportunity to change, to do better, and to improve the hostile situations that we find ourselves confronted with, whether at the personal, communal, institutional, or national level.

Acknowledging our role in interactions is essential to discovering and staying in touch with the source of our power. Our point of power as individuals is based on our self-awareness and our ability to accept the truth about ourselves and others. In exploring this idea, King cited another New Testament scripture: "Why do you see the speck in your neighbor's eye, but do not notice the log in your own eye?"[18] King described this as a tragedy of human nature. It is our tendency to be super aware of the failures and limitations of our adversaries while being woefully unaware or actively in denial about our own failures and limitations. To overturn this tendency is a difficult practice, but if we can develop our capacity to perceive ourselves and our adversaries more accurately, and even to accept them compassionately, then we begin to move into the realm of generous hospitality, extending love in the face of hostility at any level—personal, communal, institutional, or national.

SELF-EXAMINATION

Self-examination is a form of awareness practice that can help you develop your capacity for hospitality to enemies. It begins with receptivity through honest perception, but it naturally leads into the realm of reverence and compassionate acceptance if you can keep practicing it. In this exercise, you will be looking for motivating feelings and underlying attitudes that may further enmity rather than hospitality.

1. Decide how much time you want to spend on this exercise. Five to ten minutes might be all you can manage in the beginning.
2. Begin by bringing to mind a person with whom you have had hostile interactions. If there is a particular situation you can focus on, all the better. Remember the setting of that event. Whether it was at your workplace, your place of worship, book club, or bowling team, visualize the last place your saw this person. These details will help you get in touch with the memories and emotions.
3. In your imagination, remember how the person looks, dresses, and does or doesn't approach you.
4. Now, turn your attention to yourself. Notice how you feel physically while remembering this person or

situation. Notice sensations: clenching teeth? Queasy stomach? Watch whatever sensations you find for a few moments.

5. Begin to name emotional states that come up, such as anger, frustration, fear, confusion, sadness, shock, rage, grief, and so on.

6. You may find that you get distracted or lose your focus. Simply return to visualizing the physical place in which you know this individual. Once you're reconnected, you can return to contemplating your physical and emotional reactions.

7. If one emotion rises to the forefront or seems particularly potent, focus on it more directly for a while. Follow the trail of thoughts that are connected to it and ask yourself questions about it: Where is this anger coming from? What am I afraid of? Why do I feel so sad? Allow yourself to fully witness these feelings and compassionately accept that they exist in you.

8. As you practice receptivity and reverence toward yourself, your awareness may expand and your adversarial feelings may begin to loosen their grip within you. If and when this happens, you can take the next step and turn your receptive awareness toward your adversary. Can you perceive the Buddha nature or image of God deep within him or her?

9. As your time begins to draw to a close, notice any changes in how you feel here and now in relation to the person or situation you've been exploring.

Although we may react to people and events outside our control, we do have the power to understand our responses and to make choices about how we direct our thoughts and how we act. With greater self-awareness, we have more freedom to respond *pro*-actively from our point of power, rather than *re*-actively from unacknowledged human impulses. Awareness of and receptivity to ourselves and others lays the foundation for transformational hospitality.

Looking for the Evil within Us

Dr. King's second step toward loving enemies invites us to look within for a very specific purpose. He suggested that we look for the good in our enemies and look for the evil that is in us. Dr. King described us as being split up and divided against ourselves as though a civil war were raging inside us. It is the "isness" of our present nature being out of harmony with the eternal "oughtness" that forever confronts us, Dr. King said.[19] In other words, we're not as completely good as we would like to be.

If we can recognize that this is true within ourselves as well as within our adversaries, then we can no longer see ourselves as entirely innocent, or our adversaries as entirely guilty, or evil. There is no wholly good person, just as there is no wholly bad person. There are only human beings. When we can realize and remember our shared humanity with our adversaries, our attitude can shift, and a little compassion may even rise up within us.

If you would like to explore this particular practice, you can simply add a new step or focus to the earlier exercise of self-examination. Work your way through the same steps of imagining your adversary, and this time look for signs within yourself of hostility, hatred, disrespect, disdain, or anything that undermines the humanity of your adversary by seeing him or her as all bad. Also notice that seeing yourself as all good undermines your own humanity too, because that belief is not based in the complex reality of what it means to be human.

Looking for the Good in Our Adversaries

The words and labels we use for people are important in that they contain many connotations and reinforce beliefs we hold about who other people are at a fundamental level. There's something about calling a person your *enemy* that seems to concretize the hostile relationship, as well as reinforce a belief in the fundamental nature of the other's identity *as enemy*. Then it's not just how he's acting toward you that is problematic; it's his very personhood, the nature of who he is in relation to you. Such an understanding subtly but powerfully precludes a solution to the conflict, or even seeing new possibilities within the relationship.

Calling someone your *adversary* has a different effect, however. Sometimes the people we love the best are our adversaries, when we're disagreeing with them, when we're struggling, even vehemently, over some difference of opinion. An adversary is someone that we are engaging with in a certain way, in an adversarial way, but it doesn't concretize that engagement into a belief about that individual's identity. Our adversarial relationship has the potential to change into a more cooperative relationship, a more connected and less fractured relationship, even a relationship of hospitality. About this process, Dr. King said this:

> The person who hates you most has some good in him; even the nation ... [and] even the race that hates you most has some good in it. And when you come to the point that you look in the face of every man and see deep down within him what religion calls "the image of God," you begin to love him.... [Try to] find the center of goodness and place your attention there and you will take a new attitude.[20]

This is a great spiritual practice involving how we use our thoughts to affect our beliefs. Dr. King is suggesting that we place our attention not on hatred, not on evil, not on the worst in another person, but rather on the center of goodness that is surely within each and every created human being. It might be buried deep. It might be something that the person can't even perceive about herself. But looking for it with energy and commitment is a spiritual practice that can literally transform our lives because it can change how we feel, how we act, and how we understand our adversaries, ourselves, and our power and place in the world. Dr. King would take this even one step further to suggest that placing our attention on the good in our adversaries would ultimately also change them, that our love would draw that goodness out of them. That is the redemptive power of love.

A Circle of Love: Draw It Large Enough to Include Your Adversary

So how can we place our attention on the center of goodness in our adversaries? How can we begin to practice loving someone *in spite of*, as Dr. King suggests? How can we extend hospitality rather than hostility, even when hostility is directed at us? It is surely a lifelong spiritual journey to grow adept in these ways, but here is a meditative exercise that can help you practice.

The underlying goal of this exercise is to discover and remember the inherent humanity of the people with whom you are experiencing hostility and to choose to extend hospitality and love. If others are exhibiting hatred toward you, they are, in a sense, rejecting the humanity that they share with you. They are cutting you out of their circle of love and respect, but you can draw your circle big enough to keep them in it.

1. Begin by focusing on your heart as the center of your feelings of love.
2. See with your inner eye the beating of your heart. Imagine that it is pulsing with love. You might imagine the love as a certain color, or as light itself. If you need help feeling the love, you can imagine someone that you love, notice the sensation of love you feel toward him or her, and hold that sensation while releasing the image of the particular person.

3. Now imagine the light or color of love expanding to fill your whole chest, then your whole body. See it begin to extend out past the limits of your physical form and fill the whole room, then your whole town or city.

4. See the people everywhere in this area become enveloped in this light of love. Sit with this image for a few moments, allowing it to become stronger.

5. Now bring to mind an adversary and see him enveloped by this love as well. Know that the source of love is inexhaustible, enough to keep your heart pulsing with it forever. See the light permeating every part of your being, refreshing you. Imagine the same effect on the person you are holding in this light.

6. As a final step, begin to notice and focus on another light—the heart of the person you are embracing. Let her heart be the symbol of her inner center of goodness. Whatever it looks like, imagine that it, too, is beginning to glow.

7. As you watch, the light begins to expand and fill her chest, and then her body, and then extends beyond her body and surrounds you. Now the center of goodness—the light of the heart—of your adversary is surrounding you, and the light of your heart is surrounding her.

After holding this inner experience for a while, gently bring your awareness back to where you are sitting. Contemplate your experience. How does this meditation affect your feeling toward this person? The next time you are physically in her presence, remember this exercise. Bring it powerfully to mind and see whether it changes the dynamic between you.

Identify with Your Adversary

Receptivity means developing your awareness of others in addition to your awareness of your inner self. Beginning to identify with your adversaries is taking the next step beyond awareness and into compassionate acceptance. This is the realm of reverence, in which we hold together with tenderness the vulnerable fallible humanity that we all share.

When someone is acting in a hostile manner toward you, try to ask yourself what emotion she seems to be feeling. "Hatred" might be the first and easiest answer that comes up. But push yourself harder. What might she be feeling under and behind the hatred? What other emotions might the hatred be composed of? Consider whether fear, shame, powerlessness, or vulnerability might somehow be all mixed up with her hatred. Besides the emotional content, ask yourself what the mechanism might have been that caused her to act out her hostility toward you. Is there a system or experience of injustice, racism, or classism? Developing awareness of the social systems and expectations that push individuals and groups apart can help us choose to act in different ways. Getting perspective on injustice can also help us remember that some of our experiences of hostility are stemming from external situations that need to be addressed.

Whatever feelings you think might be at play in your adversary, remember times that you have felt those same emotions. Are you feeling them at the moment of the exchange with your adversary? Look for the part of you that is capable of feeling the same feelings as your adversary. This can help you identify with him, remembering your shared humanity.

Sometimes you can even gain insight into what your adversary might be feeling underneath his hostility by noting what you feel on the receiving end of his enmity. For example, if an interaction with someone leaves you feeling powerless and small, consider that he may be trying to create an illusion of power and hostility so *he* won't feel powerless and small—if you feel it, he doesn't have to. It might seem a little crazy, but this is actually a phenomenon that psychologists describe. You can test it by looking for moments in your own life when you have made yourself fell less vulnerable by acting angry at others and making *them* feel vulnerable. Identifying with the humanity of adversaries is taking the second step of hospitality, moving toward a posture of welcome and seeking to realize the inherent value or image of God within them.

DON'T BECOME AN ENEMY—PRACTICING NON-RETALIATION

This brings us to the third step recommended by Dr. King in striving to love our enemies, which is perhaps the most surprising. He said that when the opportunity arises for us to defeat our enemies, we must not do it. Non-violence seeks to defeat injustice, not people. Why must we resist defeating and demeaning people? Because hating people who hate us only increases the amount of hatred in the world.

To defeat our enemies would be to return hate for hate. It would mean becoming an enemy ourselves, increasing the evil in the world by embracing it and reproducing it ourselves. Defeat implies a kind of domination, perhaps a humiliation of our adversaries. The opportunity to defeat our enemies arises at that point when the tables turn. But if we respond to this turning of the tables by becoming dominators and transgressors ourselves, then we haven't changed the situation at all— we've only changed the players in the drama. Only one thing can end the terrible cycle of hatred, and that is love. Dr. King says that we must inject the redemptive power of love into the universe. It is the only thing that can truly conquer hate in the sense of undoing it and ending it, rather than redoing it in a new way.

Spiritual hospitality invites us to accept others as fundamentally beloved by God, flaws and all. It means remembering that the compassion God has for us, God has for our adversaries as well. In the verse from the Gospel of Matthew when Jesus says to love our enemies, he also points out that God makes the sun rise and the rain fall on evil and good people alike.[21] This points to the universality of love, and it almost rubs us the wrong way. After all, shouldn't the unrighteous and the evil suffer consequences for their wrongs? But we should note that this passage doesn't say that there are no consequences; it simply says that God treats everyone equally. The implication, when this is paired with Jesus' command to love enemies, is that God loves everybody equally. There's another well-know verse in Matthew that bears consideration on this topic of loving our enemies. In it, Jesus says, "You have heard that it was said, 'An eye for an eye and a tooth for a tooth.' But I say to you, Do not resist an evildoer. But if anyone strikes you on the right cheek, turn the other also."[22]

Was Jesus suggesting that his followers be passive and allow evil to flourish? I don't think so. Instead, he was saying don't become an enemy yourself. Don't let the hostility of others turn you into a hostile person. Don't embrace, or even accept in passing, violence as your mode of operation. This is, I believe, a call for non-retaliation. Here's a story that illustrates perfectly how the impulse to retaliation leads us into a distorted and painful life.

Once there was a samurai who sought to understand the nature of heaven and hell. When he approached a roshi for instruction, the roshi responded with harsh words. "Why should I teach an ignorant oaf like you?" The samurai began to be filled with rage while the roshi goaded him on with terrible insults. Finally, the furious samurai reached for his sword to cut off the roshi's head, and the roshi said, "That's hell."

Awareness flashed across the samurai's face as he realized how he had created and fallen into his own hell, a place where he was consumed and controlled by his own emotions. Tears sprang to his eyes as he bowed to the roshi and asked forgiveness for what he had done. The roshi said, "That's heaven."[23]

In this story, the samurai allows himself to become an enemy. By letting himself be consumed by rage, and by embracing violence as his reaction, the samurai embraces an evil impulse in himself. He is swept into a distorted world in which he is willing to kill.

SELF-DEFENSE VS. RETALIATION

Unfortunately, Jesus's admonition to "turn the other cheek" has also been used to keep the disenfranchised and disempowered in situations of degradation for long periods of history. There is a difference between physically (and possibly violently) resisting assault in self-defense and extending retaliation after an assault has occurred. Turning the other cheek is about non-retaliation, not passive acceptance of harm. Non-retaliation and nonresistance are two very different things. One can resist without retaliating.

Nelson Mandela wrote an article in 1999 about Gandhi in which he said that "Gandhi himself never ruled out violence absolutely and unreservedly. He conceded the necessity of arms in certain situations. He said, 'Where choice is set between cowardice and violence, I would advise violence ... I prefer to use arms in defense of honor rather than remain the vile witness of dishonor ...'"[24] One of the main things Gandhi taught, however, was that there are almost always alternatives to cowardice and violence—*satyagraha* being the main one.

In his autobiography, Dr. King describes some of the challenges to adopting the strategy and method of nonviolence for the civil rights movement. Some people wanted to respond to violence with violence, to "show them we're not afraid any longer." Others, King said, "felt that they could be nonviolent only if they were not attacked personally ... They thus drew a moral line between aggressive and retaliatory violence."[25] Some participants in the Montgomery bus boycott said that if they were hit, they would hit back. This represents retaliation, which King discouraged, seeing that it could pull people into terrible cycles of hostility and suffering.

There are distinctions between aggressive violence, which initiates harm; retaliatory violence, which reacts to aggression; and defensive violence, which seeks to stop violence and disengage from it. It is the disengagement that becomes incredibly difficult, because in order to disengage we have to forfeit retaliation altogether. Becoming able to let go of the impulse to return hate for hate is a major part of the practice of hospitality to enemies.

REPLACE RETALIATORY FEELINGS WITH LOVE AND COMPASSION

One way to prepare ourselves for a life of non-retaliation is to begin to separate the source of our feelings from the triggers for our feelings. Things that happen *to* us are the triggers, while the source of the feeling is *within* us. When we can make this distinction, we can begin to tap into love, forgiveness, and compassion even in the most hostile of situations. We can learn to prevent ourselves from being triggered into reactivity and instead choose how we will respond from our proactive place of power within. The following exercise can help you begin to make this distinction between sources and triggers of feelings and reactions.

1. Imagine someone you love—get in touch with how you feel about her. She is the trigger for your feelings. Focus on your emotions and allow them to grow in your awareness.

2. Now let go of her image and continue to pay attention to the feelings of love inside yourself. Notice that the love is still there inside you. The source of your feelings is inside yourself.

3. Now imagine someone you don't know or about whom you feel neutral. Holding his image in mind, remember the feelings of love. Direct those feelings toward this new person. You can do this by holding the feelings of love in the forefront of your consciousness, while you bring the image of this new person also into the forefront of your mind. Hold the person and the feelings there, together.

4. Let go of his image and continue to pay attention to the feelings of love inside yourself. Notice that the love is still there inside you. Sit with this feeling for a while, allowing yourself to be filled with it.

5. Finally, bring to mind an adversary. Notice the feelings toward her that rise up in you. Take a moment to do this.

6. Now, set aside those feelings and remember instead the feelings of love you felt toward your loved one in the beginning of this exercise.

7. Once you have the sensation of these love feelings back in mind, direct those feelings toward your adversary. Practice holding both in your mind and heart together: your feelings of love and the image of your adversary. This will take concentration, but the more you do it, the better you become at achieving it. When fear, anger, or hatred rise up, simply notice them without judging, then return to your thoughts and feelings of kindness, compassion, and love directed toward your adversary.

8. If you find it difficult to maintain the positive feelings while thinking of your adversary, return to thinking about the person or people you love. Refresh and strengthen the inner sensation of love. Then bring your adversary back to mind and direct those same feelings toward him.

When we become able to identify the internal sources of our feelings and recognize that source as different from external triggers, we develop our power to choose to stop the cycle of enmity and violence. Somebody has to be the one to step out of the cycle of returning hate for hate, and *you can be the one*. It may seem like external events are the source of our feelings, but I am making a distinction that can help us on a practical level: External things may trigger our emotions, but the true source of our feelings is internal.

Gandhi gave an example of this when he talked about reacting to a bully. When you feel humiliated by a bully, it is a natural reaction to want to slap them to "vindicate your self respect," Gandhi said. "But if you have assimilated the non-violent spirit, there should be no feeling of humiliation in you. Your non-violent behavior should then either make the bully feel ashamed of himself and prevent the insult, or make you proof against it, so that the insult would remain ... in the bully's mouth and not touch you at all."[26] Internalizing the non-violent spirit, as Gandhi put it, means detaching ourselves from the triggers of external events, so that a bully's words don't cause the harm they intend and don't trigger retaliation. Gandhi said we become "proof" against insults, like a raincoat is waterproof, or bricks are fireproof. In other words, we become bully proof.

This is not easy! But replacing retaliatory feelings with love and compassion can help us become more skillful in doing it. Gandhi went on to say that "Non-violence ... is not a mechanical thing. You do not become non-violent by merely saying, 'I shall not use force.' It must be felt in the heart.... [For] when there is that feeling it will express itself through some action. It may be a sign, a glance, even silence. But, such as it is, it will melt the heart of the wrong-doer and check the wrong."[27]

Over time, resisting the urge to defeat our enemies, resisting the urge to descend into the distortion of retaliation, begins instead to help us reach for their hands to pull them out of their own disfiguring hatred. As we strive to discover and love that which is good in them, we can begin to call out the beauty in people, turning our enemies into friends at best, or at least preventing ourselves from becoming enemies.

I WOULD RATHER DIE THAN HATE YOU

As Dr. King came to the end of his sermon in 1957, he evoked the image of looking into the eyes of everyone in Alabama, America, and the world, as he said, "'I love you. I would rather die than hate you.' And I'm foolish enough to believe that through the power of this love somewhere, men of the most recalcitrant bent will be transformed."[28]

However, it can be difficult to extend this kind of love and hospitality in the face of hostility. It's tough to remember the image of God within someone who is hurting you, especially if it seems that she *wants* to hurt you. You may try to simply shrug it off, hoping it will pass. But often the hostility won't leave you alone—you can't ignore it. You have to deal with it and attempt to move through it, because the hostility has an ongoing effect on your life. Perhaps it's an adversarial relationship with someone you love, a family member who is being confrontational, or a coworker who is lashing out at you. In those kinds of situations, your acquaintance with your adversary may make the hostility seem like even more of a betrayal. At the same time, your relationship may give you added incentive to try to address the problem by reaching through the wall of hostility and grasping some shred of love or respect that is already in place in your relationship. Dr. King described the practice like this:

> You just keep loving people and keep loving them, even though they're mistreating you. Here's the person who is a neighbor, and this person is doing something wrong to you and all of that. Just keep being friendly to that person. Keep loving them. Don't do anything to embarrass them. Just keep loving them, and they can't stand it too long. Oh, they react in many ways in the beginning. They react

with bitterness because they're mad because you love them like that. They react with guilt feelings, and sometimes they'll hate you a little more at that transition period, but just keep loving them. And by the power of your love they will break down under the load. That's love, you see. It is redemptive, and this is why Jesus says love. There's something about love that builds up and is creative. There is something about hate that tears down and is destructive. So love your enemies.[29]

This is how love begins to transform our enemies. Love interrupts the exchange of violence and highlights the violence of our adversaries. There is no justification for violating someone who loves you, someone who extends an open hand and seeks to honor you. It's risky business to return love for hate, and people have lost their lives doing it. But I wonder which situation has led to a greater loss of lives—returning love for hate, or retaliating against hatred with hatred.

Returning love for hate and offering hospitality in the face of hostility is one of the most difficult spiritual practices I know. Hostility is painful. The samurai absorbed the hostile words of the roshi and it hurt! Our choice in that situation is whether we will descend into a hell of retaliation and escalation with that person, or whether we will have the soul force to remain strong and centered in Truth, *satya*, the truth of God's love for us and for all others. Choosing to extend receptivity, reverence, and generosity rather than retaliation will bring heaven to us, here and now. Then we will be living in the realm of God, the same heaven discovered by the samurai when he bowed to the roshi.

CHAPTER SEVEN

HOSPITALITY TO CREATION

Knowing Creation Relationally

Growing up in rural New York, I was surrounded by the natural world. We lived on a dirt road in a little town called Breeseport, in a house that my father built. There I walked in the woods, played in the yard, and climbed the big maple trees around our house. One year we tapped those maple trees, drilling tiny holes in them and putting little spigots in the trunks to funnel the watery sap that flowed out of them into buckets. It tasted like woody water until we boiled down thirty gallons of it to make one gallon of maple syrup.

I knew the earth as a child knows about things, through my senses—by the smell of dirt and the feel of grass between my toes. I knew it by the bugs that bit my legs, the crickets that chirped at night, and the torturous afternoons picking wild strawberries in the field behind our house, where the tall, prickly grasses poked my arms and the sun made the sweat roll down my back. The berries were as small as raisins, red as blood, delicate, juicy and *so sweet*. I hated picking them, but I loved the strawberry shortcake that came from our harvest in the evening.

I smelled, felt, saw, tasted, and listened my way through life in the country. It was a rich embodied relationship I had with creation.

Looking back, I can see that like any relationship it was filled with joy and pain, discovery and mystery, apparent autonomy and deep reciprocity. The world and I affected each other. It affected me through berries and sunburns, bug bites and shortcakes. In my own small child-sized way, I affected the world by pulling the berries off the stems, smacking the bugs that bit me, flattening the tall grasses as I tromped through them. Sometimes my impact was less destructive, even good—like watering my mother's purple irises or feeding the chickens, whose eggs later fed us.

The world was not just an "it" to me; it wasn't just "stuff" out there. The world was part of me; it was the matrix of my life. I knew the world not as we know a thing, but as we know a complex being—relationally, reciprocally. And this is why hospitality to creation in all its forms is so important: because we interexist with it. Being receptive, reverent, and generous to creation is the same thing as being receptive, reverent, and generous to ourselves and to God, the Life of life, the source of everything. So although this is the last chapter in this book, it connects back to the beginning of the book. Having begun at the inner core with explorations of hospitality to God and the authentic self, we have arrived at the outer ring of our concentric circles of hospitality—hospitality to creation. And yet we find that here, mysteriously, the outside is inside. Through hospitality to creation we welcome God, the Life of life.

Various religions traditions speak about the relationship between God and creation in slightly different ways. Twelfth-century German mystic Abbess Hildegard of Bingen says that all creatures are like living sparks of God that show God's splendor, "just as the rays of the sun proceed from the sun itself."[1] St. Francis of Assisi has a well-known prayer in which he thanks

God, the Creator, for all God's creatures, especially the sun and the moon, who are our brothers and sisters. He calls the wind and air our brothers and the water our sister. Fire is also our brother, he says, and the earth is our sister, "who sustains and rules us, and produces different fruits with colored flowers and herbs."[2] By calling all these elements our siblings, St. Francis reveals that they are close to us, related to us, part of the "family," the network, in which we exist. They are created by and related to God, just as we are. We are all part of creation—sun, moon, wind, water, fire, earth, animals, plants, and us—part of the same family of God.

St. Francis calls our relationship to creation a family relationship, and Thich Nhat Hanh calls it a relationship of interbeing. Lao Tsu, the author of the *Tao Te Ching*, the sacred book of the followers of the Taoist religion, says, "Love the world as your own self; then you can truly care for all things."[3] I'm reminded of Jesus saying, "Love your neighbor as yourself." While the metaphors vary, they all fundamentally agree that there is an essential, vital relationship between each one of us and creation. How we act in that relationship will greatly affect the quality of our lives as well as the quality of the world and the relationship itself. Jacob Needleman, in his introduction to the *Tao Te Ching*, writes that the "fundamental forces of the cosmos itself are mirrored in our own individual, inner structure. And [the *Tao Te Ching*] invites us to try to live in direct relationship to all these forces. To see truly and to live fully: this is what it means to be authentically human."[4]

Practicing hospitality to creation can help us become more fully alive and more authentically human by helping us become aware and receptive to *what is* all around us. Needleman reflects on our human tendency, like the men and women of ancient China for whom the *Tao Te Ching* was originally written, to "try in vain to live full lives without understanding what it means to *see*. We too presume to act, to do, to create, without opening ourselves to the vision of ultimate reality."[5] There is a vision of this ultimate reality in creation; if we can become receptive, reverent, and generous toward creation, our relationship with ultimate reality will also deepen. We will become able to "truly care for all things," as Lao Tsu suggests. And in that process, we become more authentically human and more fully alive, transformed by deep spiritual hospitality.

THE CITY IS CREATION, TOO

With all my talk about chickens, wild strawberries, and fields of grasses, it's easy to lapse into thinking that creation is only the nature that exists in rural (or possibly suburban) areas. I myself can slip into this way of thinking, perhaps especially because of my rural upbringing. But the city is creation, too. Creation Spirituality theologian Matthew Fox says that nature and human nature come together to make a city.[6] After all, what is a city made of? Think of a skyscraper. It's made of steel, stone, brick, glass, and probably hundreds of other materials that I'm not aware of. But all these building materials ultimately come from the earth—it's simply that human beings have manipulated and shaped them with some skill into a really tall place to live and work.

It is human nature to make a place to live out of the materials of nature. Divine creativity and human creativity come together in the creation of a city. Unfortunately, we forget this all too easily and begin to think that cities are solely the work of human ingenuity and industry, and thereby lose touch with the ultimate reality that this form of nature, or creation, can also reveal. We forget about the role of creation itself, the forces of Life, of nature, or the power of a Creator Spirit who brings us granite and iron, coal and clay.

Expanding our awareness may help us see the sacred in our cities. Hopefully, it will also lead us to experience reverence and commit ourselves to create and live in our cities in ways that will affirm and refresh life rather than deny and deplete life. But we'll come back to that point later. First, let's just work with receptivity and awareness and experiment with seeing creation in a city. If you would like to actively explore that idea, you can direct your awareness practice to some of the human-made machines and buildings in a city. But if you don't live in a city, you can try this paradigm-shifting exercise in any town or even at a mall in the suburbs. All you need is a place with machines (cars count), buildings, or anything "created" by human beings.

1. **Choose the object that you'll focus on**—a building, a car, a road, a street light. For the purposes of this illustration, I'll focus this example on my urban apartment building.

2. **Consider the physical elements in the object of your focus.** In my apartment, I notice red brick, wooden floors, a metal gas stove, furniture with fabrics and stuffing and wooden frames and so on. Each one of these elements in my apartment could become the focus of an in-depth contemplation. I'll focus on the building structure itself, because it's so big.

3. **Ask yourself where these materials come from.** For example, what are the elements that come together to make the brick of my apartment? Some of the bricks are red and some yellow, some with coarse surfaces that look like clay, and some with finer surfaces that look like fine sand. Clearly, these bricks come from the earth. As dirt, sand, or clay, these bricks come from other processes of life—growth and decay—as plants and animals become dirt, and rock becomes sand, and sedimentation creates clay, and so on.

4. **Consider the efforts and processes required to get the raw material into the form it is in now.** How did earth become the two-story brick building in which I now

live? I recently gained a little insight into the creation of bricks. My dad, who is a carpenter in his heart of hearts, is nevertheless working in masonry right now. He took me on a tour of the brick-production plant that his crew is currently constructing. They built it from bricks! The plant walls are constructed of thousands of bricks, laid by hand, and inside are long hallways built of fireproof bricks that will become the actual kilns to harden more bricks. The plant, when it is finished, will be powered by methane gas generated by decay at a nearby dump. Wherever and whenever the bricks for my apartment building were created, they required hundreds of workers, tons of earth, and many other natural resources, including energy sources and people-hours. If these bricks could talk, they would have stories to tell. Some of them we might just hear, if we listen and look a little more closely.

In doing this exercise, hopefully we may come to see that all things interexist, even things that seem straightforward, singular, and autonomous, like a building. There is no such thing as independence in creation, from the untouched wilderness to an urban street. So, while Thich Nhat Hanh speaks about clouds, sun, earth, and rain coming together to be a flower, we can also see the many elements that come together to be a city building. Through this awareness exercise we can change our focus and even our paradigm in order to remember that divine creation is present in all the things that we human beings create.

This awareness, in turn, helps us show hospitality to creation, whether that is in a city environment, a rural environment, or something in between. Developing a specific understanding of all the resources and factors going into the creation of our homes, transportation, and communication systems will help us clearly see just how our choices affect ourselves and the world itself—creation in all its complexity.

In addition to developing our awareness of urban and human-made things, we can continue developing our awareness of nature in its more wild state. Georgia O'Keeffe, who is famous for painting huge canvases of flowers, said that "nobody sees a flower—really—it is so small—we haven't time—and to see takes time, like to have a friend takes time." She said that if she painted what she saw in a small flower, her painting would be small too, and no one would look at it. So instead, she said, "I'll paint it big and they will be surprised into taking time to look at it—I will make even busy New Yorkers take time to see what I see of flowers."[7]

Not only did she make busy New Yorkers look at what she saw of flowers, she also made it possible for busy Chicagoans to see it too, and busy people as far as her fame later carried her images. O'Keeffe took the time to look deeply at flowers (and many other things, too). Developing this awareness is partly a matter of taking time, as she said. But I think that it's equally important to empty our hearts and minds of our notions that animals or plants or any part of creation is somehow less important than people are. A flower can point us to the ultimate reality, but many of us suffer from a lack of reverence for the inherent value and sacredness in creation. Getting that reverence back is an essential part of developing the capacity to offer hospitality to creation.

Receptivity means making time available for opening to, looking into, and knowing creation. But to get from receptivity to reverence means making our hearts available to really care. These are the twin practices of receptivity and reverence—making ourselves available to know through attentiveness, and making ourselves available to love, which flows naturally out of a deep knowing. Sally McFague, author of *Super, Natural Christians*, writes about the interconnected quality of receptivity and reverence. She says, "To *really* love nature (and not just our-selves in nature or nature as useful to us—even its use as a path-way to God), we must pay attention *to it*. Love and knowledge go together; we can't have the one without the other."[8]

REVERENCE FLOWS FROM RECEPTIVITY

Across the road from the house my father built, there was a stream that a family of beavers dammed up to make a little pond for themselves. They were building their house just as my father had built ours when I was four years old. He bull-dozed earth to level a spot for our cement foundation, and the wooden beams going up became the skeleton of our home. The beavers gnawed trees down with their teeth and dragged them into the middle of their new pond to pile them into their twiggy house. We could see the teeth marks on the short stand-ing stumps they left behind. We could also see them swim-ming, their noses sticking out of the water, a small wake trailing out behind them in the shape of a V. I suppose they could see us too, walking up and down the long driveway to get the mail from the box by the road, mowing the lawn, plant-ing vegetables in the garden.

I loved the beavers. They were a mystery to me. How could their teeth be that strong? What did the inside of their house look like? On the outside it looked like a pile of sticks and branches. How did they know to build a dam? Didn't they get cold in the water? I knew I did, if I stayed in too long. They were like mysterious strangers to me. All I could do was watch them in wonder and love them with my child's heart.

By spending time watching and wondering about the beavers, I was able to see the miracle and diversity of life and to be awed by it. Looking back on the experience now, I can see that I related to them as a being relates to other beings: caring about them, wanting to know them better.

Jewish scholar Martin Buber explores this way of knowing in his classic book, *I and Thou*. It is a deep philosophical exploration of the intrinsic relationality of existence.[9] He says that there are two essential attitudes that we as human beings can hold toward the world: We can relate to what we encounter as "It" or we can relate to what we encounter as "You." Relating to something as "It" doesn't just mean tables and chairs; we can also make people into Its. When we relate to things or people in this way, we experience them, but we don't really encounter them. We may see them, we may know their names, but we don't really *know* them. We're not really in relationship with whomever or whatever we experience as an It. Buber seems to suggest that we give up a little bit of our humanity when we are in these kinds of "I-It" relationships. When we make people and things into Its, we also become more like an It ourselves.

But there's another way that we can be. We can relate to others not as an It, but as a "You." When we relate in this way, we don't just experience others; we begin to know them and enter into an "I-You" relationship. We are one kind of person when we are having *I-It experiences* and a different kind of person when we are in *I-You relationships*. This means that how we treat the world will change who we are. If we are hospitable to the world, we will be in an I-You relationship with it. That kind of relationship includes elements of receptivity, reverence, and generosity, as any truly hospitable encounter does. But if we treat the world as a collection of minerals, plants, and animals to be used up for our benefit, then we are living in an I-It experience and we never really fully know the world; we never really understand the deep sacredness that permeates creation and flows through us as a part of that creation. To live in the world as I-It begins to deplete us and disconnect us from the very source of life.

Martin Buber explored the differences between the I-It experience and the I-You relationship in his contemplation of a tree.

I contemplate a tree.

I can accept it as a picture: a rigid pillar in a flood of light, or splashes of green traversed by the gentleness of the blue silver ground.

I can feel it as movement: the flowing veins around the sturdy, striving core, the sucking of the roots, the breathing of the leaves ...

I can assign it to a species ... I can overcome its uniqueness and form ... I can dissolve it into a number ...

Throughout all of this the tree remains my object and has its place and its time span, its kind and condition.

But it can also happen, if will and grace are joined, that as I contemplate the tree I am drawn into a relation, and the tree ceases to be an It ...

Whatever belongs to the tree is included: its form and its mechanics, its colors and its chemistry, its conversation with the elements and its conversation with the stars—all this in its entirety.

The tree is no impression, no play of my imagination, no aspect of mood; it confronts me bodily and has to deal with me as I must deal with it—only differently.

One should not try to dilute the meaning of the relation: relation is reciprocity.

Does the tree have consciousness, similar to our own? I have no experience of that ... What I encounter is neither the soul of a tree nor a dryad, but the tree itself.[10]

In this exercise, Buber practiced receptivity, then went beyond it into reverence. First, he became broadly aware of the tree, inviting perception at a level deeper than the mere surface. Then he moved into the realm of reverence when he allowed the tree to become a You. He welcomed a relational encounter in which the tree was no longer a mere object, but a You to be known. Buber would describe this as participation in the world, rather than a mere experience of It. The participation carries us beyond the inner self into a space between I and You,[11] a place where we exist together, in relationship. I-You signifies relationship and reciprocity. This is the "with" phase of hospitality—a true encounter and welcome, in this case a reverent welcome of the sacredness of creation.

Being hospitable to creation begins with holding a receptive heart toward life around us. It means having that "poverty" of heart that we've explored in earlier chapters, which creates an empty or available space inside us into which others may enter. In this case, we let what is outside us—creation, the natural world—come inside our awareness and even our hearts. This kind of receptivity allows us to know more deeply and then to love more reverently. And if we love the world, we'll want to protect it and serve it—especially if there is a little piece of it that we really personally love. Sally McFague makes this point, that it's easier to love a little piece of earth—a particular park, say—than it is to love the planet, the blue marble photographed from space.[12] This means focusing on the here and now and acting from the point of power within us. It includes interacting with creation as it comes into our presence and awareness, much as we respond to the neighbors who come into our path. To see garbage strewn throughout the park that we like to sit in, or piling up along the streets we walk down, may inspire more passion from us than the garbage that we "hear about" in other places.

The adage "think globally, act locally" was coined to help us remember that our local actions have global consequences. It reminds us of our interdependence and even our interbeing. The "act locally" part is crucial because it reminds us that even little efforts can add up and make a difference in the big picture, which could otherwise paralyze us into inaction. Acting locally keeps us engaged locally, keeps us seeing where and how our efforts make a difference. See the world, love the world, nurture the world. That's hospitality in-with-out.

The *Tao Te Ching* reminds us to keep things on a human scale, a doable scale. "In the universe the difficult things are done as if they are easy. In the universe great acts are made up of small deeds. The sage does not attempt anything very big, and thus achieves greatness."[13]

PRACTICE SEEING CREATION WITH REVERENCE

Growing into an adult, I lost some of my capacity to see with wonder and relate to the world around me with love, as I did with the beavers when I was a child. I stopped paying attention to the fascinating mystery of life and the joyful, sometimes frightening enterprise of full encounter with another. I notice this when I think of myself and other adults with children who are encountering animals that are new to them. The children's eyes light up the way mine did for the beaver, while we adults comment on how cute the child is to feel this way. Maybe if we looked at penguins, or rabbits, or ducks, or even city pigeons with a child's open heart we would begin to perceive the miracle of life more clearly. Maybe our eyes would light up too, and we would feel reverence for the fundamental sacredness in the living beings around us.

In fact, this is something that we can still do by redirecting some of our energy. We can actively choose to engage creation with hospitality in ways that stretch us and help us regain some of the embodied reverence that we have lost. Here are some ideas to help you begin.

- **Open the "child's eye" within you. Go looking at things with rapt attention.** Children can be our teachers in this. If you have children in your life, you can invite them to go with you on a journey to explore the mysteries of your block or the park or your yard or the zoo. Only this time, instead of watching them experience joy, try to see what they see. Whether or not you have a child you can bring with you, you can find the child inside you.

- **Wonder about the experience of nonhuman animals. Make a list of your questions.** Some examples are: What is the inside of a beaver's house like? How do fish remember things? (For example, how do my tropical fish know to swim toward me when I walk up to their tank to look at them? They seem to remember that I feed them.) How does the world look to a bird, since their eyes are on opposite sides of their head? Also, consider what the animals all around you need for their well-being. They need many of the same things you do—clean air, water, food, places to sleep. Sometimes their needs may conflict with yours, like when that bird wants to live in the tree you want to cut down, or the dam that will create a reservoir of drinking water for humans floods a habitat. How do you feel about that? Considering the experience of animals can help you value their existence with reverence—a precursor of generosity, and an important element of hospitality.

- **Notice that life is happening all around you and it's not about you** or where you're going or what you need to get accomplished today. Take some time to let go of your adult thoughts and simply be. Notice the whirligig seedpods that fall out of trees. Notice that they are whirligigs. Count how many colors of flowers you can see. Notice the different kinds of bark that grows on different kinds of trees. Touch it. Look for the Life of life in a tree. Consider that this creation is not a collection of props on the stage of your life—rather, all that you encounter affects you and is affected by you. Make time in your life and space in your heart to remember and to feel this.

GENEROSITY: EMBODYING A LIFE OF BALANCE WITH CREATION

In all cases of hospitality, what flows out of us is an enactment of our desire for the well-being of others—this is the generosity that completes the cycle of hospitality. It is true of our hospitality to creation as well. To be generous is to give, not to consume. We may receive unexpected gifts or blessings from those we serve, but we don't take from them. Generosity is doing what needs to be done, or at least whatever we are capable of doing (which is probably a bit more than we think we are capable of) to ensure the well-being of those we come to know and love through receptivity and reverence.

Recalling St. Francis's metaphor of the creatures and elements of creation as our sisters and brothers, we can consider our generosity toward creation by thinking about how we treat our actual sisters and brothers when we are in right relationship with them. When eating together with brothers and sisters, we share food; we don't take all their food and leave them hungry. When living together, we don't throw our garbage into their bedrooms. We don't take all their clothing or all their money to use for ourselves, leaving them without. On the contrary, we make sure that we each have the basics for getting by. And if we are being hospitable toward them and extending generosity, we give them more than the basics. We give whatever we can and maybe a little more than we thought we could.

Using up the world's resources is the opposite of extending hospitality; it is being a terrible guest. Or, to stick with the metaphor of family, this is being the sister or brother who eats up all the food, "borrows" other people's clothes, runs up the phone bill, leaves the gas tank on empty, and uses the last piece of toilet paper without replacing the roll. With regard to (mis)treating creation in this way, none of us means to be doing this. Many of us are just not aware of the impact that our day-to-day decisions have on the rest of the world. Or, when we do become aware, we may easily become overwhelmed because we are part of big systems over which we seem to have no control. It is a natural tendency in a moment like this to want to look the other way rather than acknowledge the sensations we feel. But rather than looking away, we can look for our "point of power" and identify what it is that we *can* change. What is it that we can affect—our particular neighborhood parks? Our personal use of electricity or other resources?

Our individual actions may not immediately solve the problem of planetary climate change, but we can change ourselves, and through that, slowly, culture begins to change, too. We can become people of hospitality toward creation. We can become awake, aware, receptive to the truth of sacredness in creation. And being awake to it means that we will be more deeply in relationship with it. We will feel the sacredness and reverence begin to permeate our own lives in greater ways. And this sense of the sacred, of reverence and love, can give us the impulse and the commitment to live a life more and more in balance with the rest of creation, using only our fair share of resources, without depleting the earth. "Relation is reciprocity," Martin Buber said, and so in the "currents of universal reciprocity,"[14] our relationship with creation is one of both host and guest. We are all intimately connected.

Recently I was sitting in the woods in western Michigan, looking up a hill. Sunlight reached the ground only in splashes between leaves. Everywhere else, the light caught in leaves, glowing through them, a vibrant translucent green. Sitting there, my shoulders relaxed, my breathing deepened, my awareness broadened. I felt part of the natural world, at home with the rustling of leaves, the cawing and chirping of birds. I remembered that I am not the center of the universe, but that I am an integral part of it. I felt connected, related.

A blue jay landed quite close to me and began pecking in the sandy soil with his beak. He was looking for food, I imagined. He flitted to the roots of another tree, then another, pecking, pecking, flinging dirt from side to side as he searched persistently for bugs. How and why might I extend hospitality to this blue jay? How am I already related to it? I know in my mind that we are all interconnected, but understanding that at a deeper level is harder. At a theoretical level I realize: no bugs, no bird. I don't eat the bugs the blue jay eats, but those bugs do die and decay and become the earth from which my lettuce grows. No bugs, no lettuce. So, although it may seem that my life would be just the same with or without the blue jay, my life and my lettuce depend upon the links of the food chain staying connected. I need the bugs and all sorts of life to die and decay in order for new life to come out of them.

When I am not sitting in the rural woods of Michigan, I am living in my tiny urban apartment and have to work a little harder to stay in touch with these natural processes of life and death and new life. When I lived in the county we had a compost pile, which I found simply miraculous. We threw our food waste in a big fenced-in pile near our garden, along with a little dirt, grass clippings, and dead leaves. Months later it had transformed into beautiful, rich, fertile soil to be tossed into our garden to make our vegetables grow.

I watch a similar process of decay and new life—through the transition of garbage into dirt and into plants—by keeping a worm composting bucket under my kitchen counter. Yes, they're live worms! But don't be alarmed; more and more people are doing it, and the worms stay well contained in their little habitat. As an urban apartment dweller, I find this one way to stay in touch with the natural processes of compost—that great miracle of God. From death, new life comes. I place my broccoli stumps and assorted vegetable peels in the composting bucket, stir them up with shredded paper, red worms that love the compost habitat, and a little dirt. After a few months, I have a bucket of rich, fertile soil. "Worm castings," technically, which means, yes, it's worm dung. Tell that to a ten-year-old. He'll love it. I have a bucket of worm dung in my kitchen. But really, it just looks and smells like fresh dirt, ready to be mixed in with other soil and sprinkled on my houseplants and potted tomato plants. When I harvest the worm castings, I leave the worms in the bucket, just waiting for fresh broccoli stumps. Is this hospitality? Feeding my worms in order to make rich wholesome dirt in order to feed my plants?

I think it *is* a practice of hospitality to creation. Henri Nouwen suggests that "it is not in self-sufficiency but in creative interdependency that the mystery of life unfolds itself to us."[15] In this case, I see the creation of life out of death, and the interdependency of my waste as the food of worms and the worms' waste as instrumental in creating my food. This may be perfectly logical in a science classroom, but in my kitchen it continues to be a miracle. The mystery of life unfolds itself to me when I am this close to it. Suddenly, I see it in a new way, a more embodied way, a sensory way. And because my body and my life are engaged in this creative reenactment of life and death, it reminds me that I am alive, and that I am connected to forces so much greater than myself.

We can practice hospitality by embodying our generosity toward creation—by living more lightly on the planet, becoming aware of and challenging our tendency to overconsume like a greedy guest depleting the household. We can leave more resources for other creatures (human or otherwise) to use, allowing the earth to replenish itself by giving back in equal measure what we use for our own well-being.

PRACTICE SIMPLE LIVING AS EMBODIMENT OF HOSPITALITY TO CREATION

Offering generosity to creation means nurturing it to flourish. Sometimes it requires us to give a little more than we think we are able, or to shift our focus off of our own comfort and seek instead the well-being of the world. Becoming a person of deep hospitality often means changing the shape of our lives, changing our priorities, and learning new ways of being. Extending hospitality to creation is no exception. If you would like to begin to practice, here are a few things to consider, as well as some resources to help you go deeper.

- **Sign up to receive eco-tips by e-mail.** There are several organizations that are committed to sharing this kind of information and have lots of ideas for simple things you can do that add up to make quite a difference in the long run. A tip-of-the-day or tip-of-the-month in your e-mail box can keep the issue and concern in the forefront of your mind and encourage you in your practice of receptivity, reverence, and generosity toward creation. One such service is provided by www.greenoptions.com, which describes itself as a community dedicated to environmental resources, education, and discussion.
- **Examine your impulses to acquire more of anything.** In response to people complaining about how much stuff and clutter they have in their lives, my meditation teacher said that it's not our stuff that gives us the greatest problem; it's our addiction to dealing in stuff. I resisted this idea at first. After all, I don't ask for all the junk mail I get. I don't ask for the excessive packaging that things come in. But as I continued to contemplate her comment, I began to see the truth in it. Although I don't "ask" for the junk mail I get, there are lots of other ways that I clutter my life with possessions that only capture my imagination for a short time. I purchase household items because they're prettier than the things I already have. I purchase food that I think I

want, but then half of it spoils in the fridge because I don't take the time to cook it. So, to engage this idea when you are about to acquire one more thing, ask yourself, "Why do I want this? How will the quality of my life be affected if I don't purchase this? Can I really use this in a timely manner?" You can also reduce your incoming mail clutter by registering with the National Do Not Mail List at www.directmail.com, or by getting off mailing lists through the Direct Marketing Association at www.the-dma.org. Yes, you can actually ask *not* to get junk mail!

• **Take care of things. Reduce, reuse, recycle, rethink.** I've noticed an impulse in myself and in my friends and family to have new things. There's something a bit exciting about having something new. We imagine that new things will look better, work better, and somehow improve our lives. Often they cause us to throw away things that aren't as shiny and new, or they just add to the clutter that slowly builds up in our homes.

Rethinking our relationship and extending hospitality to creation includes looking for the value in objects and caring for them. With abundant access to "stuff" and a society that encourages a mentality of consumerism, it's easy to fall into treating objects and resources carelessly. Instead of caring less, you can care more. Reverence and generosity together are equivalent to caring emotionally and caring physically. Take the time to clean something up and rethink how to reuse it instead of just buying more.

• **Think about your food, where it comes from, and what's in it.** There's a website at www.localharvest.com where you can search by zip code to find locally grown, organic foods near you. Community Supported Agriculture (CSA) is a system developed to support farmers to grow organic and diverse foods that nourish the earth as well as us. Basically, you the customer buy a share of the farm's produce in advance to guarantee that the farmer will have an income. They then grow the food and deliver your share to you (or you pick it up). Another great resource that allows you to search for your area by zip code is www.earth911.org. At that site, you'll be able to access lots of information about everything from energy and air quality to cars and composting.

- **How about keeping live worms in your kitchen!?** Do you feel ready to invite and welcome them into your home? You can order a ready-to-go vermi-composting (worm-composting) bin like mine from www.wormwoman.com. It comes with an instruction booklet and a pound of the special red worms that love to live in compost. Make some worms happy—feed them your garbage. And if you have more space than some of us city dwellers, you could consider an actual compost pile or bin.

- **Make greener choices.** *Consumer Reports* has put together a special website at www.greenerchoices.org, where you can find links to many sites with educational resources about environmental topics, renewable energy sources, and recycling tips. It includes many links to sites that will help you understand how much impact your lifestyle is making on the environment—yes, that's *your* lifestyle. Keep it personal and keep it real. Changing our own lives, here and now, is what will change the culture over time.

- **Work to reduce your environmental impact. Be a more respectful guest on the planet. Be a more generous host to creation.** Begin with easy things, like turning off the lights more often, only boiling as much water as you actually need for your tea, washing your clothing in cold water more often, turning off your electronic equipment when you're not using it. It seems small, but it truly adds up. I was shocked one summer when I was working as an intern in an urban church. After I was there for a month, the pastor asked me what I was doing with the electricity; our electric bill had plummeted. But I really wasn't doing anything that extraordinary. Since I was often the last one to leave the building, I was just making sure that all the lights in the classrooms and the sanctuary were turned off at night.

• **Learn about "carbon footprints" and "carbon offsets."** The Greener Choices website can help you get started with this. There are more and more ways to make positive contributions to the health of our planet. Networks and organizations have been set up to help people do just this. For example, to counteract the negative effects of the carbon emissions from driving a car, you can purchase wind-generated electricity. We can begin right now giving something back to the earth, and begin creating a market for things like alternative sources of fuel.

• **Consider the spiritual implications of "going green."** Quaker Earthcare Witness (QEW) provides one interesting resource that addresses this side of going green. QEW is "a spiritually centered movement of Quakers and like-minded people seeking ways to integrate concern for the environment with Friends' long-standing testimonies for simplicity, integrity, peace, and equality." For example, speaker Ted Bernard described at a Quaker retreat the testimony of integrity as "a commitment to truth, honesty, authenticity, and wholeness, which implies a life more fully integrated into the workings of creation—that of God in every living thing."[16] You can read more at their website, www.quakerearthcare.org.

- **Learn about and join interfaith efforts to express hospitality to creation.** More and more interfaith organizations are making efforts to organize and empower
people to live more generously and respectfully on our
earth. One is Faith in Place, based in Chicago, which
says that two of the things shared by all faiths are a
call to love one another and to honor creation; see
www.faithinplace.org. The National Council of
Churches, an ecumenical network of Christian
churches, has lots of helpful information at their
website, www.nccecojustice.org. There is also a
website for the Alliance of Religions and Conservation
(www.arcworld.org), which features information about
the ecological efforts of eleven different faiths: Baha'i,
Buddhism, Christianity, Daoism (Taoism), Hinduism,
Islam, Jainism, Judaism, Shintoism, Sikhism, and
Zoroastrianism. One project of the Alliance of
Religions and Conservation is the Sacred Land Project,
which is about reminding people that the landscape
where they live can be as sacred as any holy land.

Hospitality to creation begins with receptivity—an invitation for
true encounter extended from our authentic self. Opening our
awareness to the world around us is one way to develop our
capacity to experience such receptivity. Catholic priest Henri
Nouwen said, "All nature conceals its deepest secret and cannot
reveal its hidden wisdom and profound beauty if we do not listen carefully and patiently."[17] Encountering the profound beauty
of creation causes reverence to blossom in us. How could we not
love something so beautiful, once we see that beauty?

Engaging with creation all around us—whether in our
cities, the untamed wilderness, or anything in between—as a
You and not an It will begin to transform our relationship
into one of hospitality. Through reverence, receptivity, and

generosity, we can move beyond mere experience of the planet into the realm of knowing creation, not as we know a thing, but as we know a complex being with whom we are in a reciprocal relationship. We are deeply interconnected, whether as sparks emanating from God, as Hildegard of Bingen would say, or as the family of God, according to St. Francis.

HOSPITALITY: THE JOURNEY CONTINUES

Today I went for a walk with no destination. This was actually quite difficult for me. I alternated between hovering in my doorway and rushing back into my apartment looking for things to do. I checked my wallet to see if I needed to go to the bank while I was walking around. I looked in the fridge—did I need to buy anything at the corner market? Not really.

My doctor told me that I need to walk in the sunshine at least fifteen minutes a day because my vitamin D levels are down. What a great instruction from a doctor! Walk in the sunshine. But how could that be my only purpose? The world is filled with so many things to accomplish, so many errands to complete. Yet I had been given a new purpose: encounter the sun. Make space in my life for light. So when I finally left the house my only destination was sunshine.

It was one of those final days of summer, warm but not too hot. It was late in the afternoon, so I walked west toward the sun as it hovered near the tops of the city buildings and shone directly into the street down which I was walking. I zigzagged through the neighborhood, purposely choosing the streets that had the most sunlight shining in long stretches down sidewalks, reflecting off walls and glowing luminously through the leaves on the trees.

I passed a tall fence covered so lushly with vines and vibrant greenery that I stopped to look more closely at the leaves, their veins, and their slightly curled edges.

Refocusing my eyes, I looked through the greenery into the yard behind it and there sat an older gentleman, also taking in the sunshine. I was startled, but he just smiled and nodded. For a moment we were completely together in the afternoon sun. I nodded and smiled in return and then continued on my journey.

Time seemed to slow down, extending hospitality toward me, offering me a free and open space in which to be nurtured. My breathing slowed also, and became deeper. I wasn't just killing time or squeezing as many activities as possible into it. Rather, I was being hospitable to time—actually experiencing time, receptively and reverently. In it, I was encountering my neighborhood and my neighbors more deeply. And in this way, I was experiencing my self and creation more hospitably, too.

Hospitality means embracing the abundance of life, not in the sense of collecting and consuming material things, but in the sense of being *alive* in relationships that are available everywhere you turn—family, friends, neighbors, strangers, and even enemies and creation itself. How you move through those relationships is based on the choices you make—and you have the capacity to make different choices at any time. You can grow and change by keeping in mind and putting into practice the in-with-out paradigm that we've explored in this book:

- You can look deeply to develop awareness and understanding to become more *receptive* and invitational.
- You can empty your heart of preconceived notions and allow your heart to know and love in new ways. You can develop *reverence* and a welcoming presence.
- You can act from the place of power within you—responding rather than reacting, offering tangible physical, emotional, and spiritual nurture with a *generosity* greater than you imagined you could.

Hospitality begins in the center of yourself—in the inner sanctuary where you encounter a God of life and love who embraces you. In this place, God and the true self come together, whether we call that coming together the presence of the image of God or the state of interbeing. Hospitality changes us, bringing us closer to our own authentic and true selves that are filled with the potential to love. Practicing hospitality in that center allows the image of God, our potential, to become the likeness of God as we begin to share the deep welcome that we have first received from that God in whom we live and move and have our being. Practicing transformative spiritual hospitality is what Episcopal priest Stephanie Spellers describes as "radical welcome." It is "about finding yourself utterly accepted and embraced by God, and then running into the world and your community to see how you could extend that hospitality to others."[18]

When we make choices to become more hospitable, we find that we become more whole ourselves—open to the world, to life, to relationship. Living centered in hospitality is living centered in love, trust, possibility, and hope. When we allow God and true self to come together in our inner core, we find ourselves filled with a love that we can't help but share. It overflows from within us—touching our families, neighbors, strangers, enemies, and creation itself with receptive, reverent, and generous hospitality.

I hope that your journey into the free and open spaces of hospitality will have just such a quality. May invitation, welcome, and nurture overflow your heart.

A C K N O W L E D G M E N T S

There are so many people to thank, people who have made this book possible by the care and support that they have given me, as well as the vision of hope and possibility that they have offered.

First of all, I thank my parents for inviting, welcoming, and nurturing me into this world, and my sisters and brother for being my first family. I thank my nieces and nephews for helping me become a better person by learning to become a better aunt.

Thank you, Ani Tuzman, for being a sister lover-of-God and for taking me in when I needed a home; and thank you Naomi, Emmanuel, and Melah, for loving me and letting me love you. To Eily, LaDonna, Allen, Kerry, Sarah, thank you for modeling hospitality and generosity so beautifully. To Aja, thank you for sharing so much of your life with me; you are part of my family forever. To Andres, Sharon, Joel, Benny, Liz, and Bob—you're the best.

Thanks to Burns Stanfield, who served me communion for the first time, and to the members of Fourth Presbyterian Church in Boston, who nurtured me, baptized me, and helped me become a pastor. Thank you, Matthew Myer Boulton, for making the pivotal invitation to church and showing me the best side of Christianity. Thanks to John B. Carmen, Jon Levenson, Sarah Coakley, and Diana Eck, teachers who made my world bigger, taught me how much I don't know, and showed me how to go about finding out a little bit more. Thanks to my teachers, friends, and colleagues at McCormick Theological Seminary, for walking with me on the journey and helping me join in the dynamic, creative chorus that is Christianity.

Thank you, Janie Spahr, for teaching me through your words and your ways how to step into the fullness of who I am— I am still learning. To my friends and colleagues in the Mystical Church Network, Jud, Karen, Jen, Won, Kelly, and Corey S., thank you for your words and prayers and touch and play and all the ways you help me *be*.

To my editor, Mark Ogilbee, without whose skill, sensitivity, and support this book would surely not exist: thank you, thank you, thank you. Kathryn Casey, Mark W. Wendorf, and Clare Butterfield, thanks for reading drafts and sharing your insightful responses. Thanks to Ivan M. Granger of Poetry Chaikhana for helping me track down Hildegard of Bingen poetry. Thank you to my friends in the emerging and emergent church—you give me hope. Thanks for being in conversation and friendship with me.

I am filled with gratitude for Wicker Park Grace, where I am honored to be in community and on a spiritual journey. Thanks for slogging through early drafts of this book and encouraging me to keep writing anyway. Thank you for sharing with me your passions, hopes, dreams, honest struggles, and brilliant insights. Thank you for cocreating and coleading with me a community of hospitality.

I thank all my teachers everywhere, known and unknown, for helping me to learn and grow: my friends, family, neighbors, strangers, enemies, creation, the Holy One who speaks to me in love, and the inner Self, who whispers to me when I take care to listen (and sometimes when I don't). Thank you.

NOTES

FOREWORD
1. Kathleen Norris, *Dakota: A Spiritual Geography* (New York: Houghton Mifflin, 1993), 191.

CHAPTER ONE
1. Meister Eckhart, *Meister Eckhart: A Modern Translation*, trans. Raymond Bernard Blakney (New York: Harper & Row, 1941), 180.
2. Hildegard of Bingen, *Symphonia: A Critical Edition of the Symphonia Armonie Celestium Revelationum*, trans. Barbara Newman (Ithaca, NY: Cornell University Press, 1998), 143.
3. Ibid., 148–151. The Latin for these portions reads: "O iter fortissimum, quod penetravit omnia in altissimis et in terrenis et in omnibus abyssis, tu omnes componis et colligis. De te nubes fluunt, ether volat, lapides humorem habent, aque rivulos educunt, et terra viriditatem sudat." Though English translations add the word "people," the Latin seems to suggest that the force of the fiery Spirit gathers and binds all creation, especially as the phrase is followed by a poetic reflection on clouds, wind, rain, and stone.
4. Karen Armstrong offers an in-depth exploration of various ideas and ways of talking about God in her book *A History of God: The 4,000 Year Quest of Judaism, Christianity and Islam* (New York: Ballantine Books, 1993). It's not just the mystics who talk about God as the matrix of Life. Even Thomas Aquinas, the great Christian theologian, describes God as not a Being, but as Being Itself (*esse seipsum*). According to Armstrong, Aquinas also addressed the difficulty of talking about or understanding God when he wrote, "Hence in the last resort all that man knows of

God is to know that he does not know him, since he knows that what God is surpasses all that we can understand of him." Armstrong interprets Aquinas as intending that "God cannot be anything like the beings we know but rather their ground or the condition for their existence." *A History*, 205–206.

5. Shunryu Suzuki, *Zen Mind, Beginner's Mind: Informal Talks on Zen Meditation and Practice* (New York: Weatherhill, 1970), 66.

6. Acts 17:28.

7. Thich Nhat Hanh, *Living Buddha, Living Christ* (New York: Riverhead Books, 1995), 39.

8. Diana Butler Bass, *Christianity for the Rest of Us: How the Neighborhood Church Is Transforming the Faith* (San Francisco: HarperSanFrancisco, 2006), 87.

9. Kallistos Ware, "An Interview with Bishop Kallistos Ware," by James Moran, in *Parabola: The Magazine of Myth and Tradition*, vol. X, no. 1 (February 1985), 63.

10. Martin Buber, *The Way of Response* (New York: Schocken Books, 1966), 131.

11. Ibid., 136.

12. Thich Nhat Hanh, *Being Peace* (Berkeley: Parallax Press, 1987), 28.

13. Galatians 2:20, New Revised Standard Version.

14. Martin Buber, *I and Thou* (New York: Simon & Schuster, 1996), 67.

15. Clifton Wolters, trans., *The Cloud of Unknowing and Other Works* (London: Penguin Books, 1961), 67.

16. Thomas Keating, *Open Mind, Open Heart* in *Foundations for Centering Prayer and the Christian Contemplative Life* (New York: Continuum, 2002), 8.

17. These instructions are paraphrased, but you can find the original in Thomas Keating, *Foundations for Centering Prayer*, 118–199.

18. Psalm 139, New Living Translation.

19. Thich Nhat Hanh, *Peace Is Every Step: The Path of Mindfulness in Everyday Life* (New York: Bantam Books, 1991), 23–24.

20. This is common in many Hindu temples, which have an inner room called the *garbha griha*, the "womb-house," which is also often translated as the womb-chamber. The Jewish First Temple of Solomon and the Second Temple in Jerusalem also had an inner sanctuary called the Holy of Holies where only the high priest could enter.

21. Anthony de Mello, *Sadhana, A Way to God: Christian Exercises in Eastern Form* (New York: Image Books, 1984), 78.
22. Abraham Joshua Heschel, *The Sabbath* (New York: Farrar, Straus and Giroux, 1951), 16.

CHAPTER TWO

1. Father Daniel Homan, O.S.B, and Lonni Pratt, *Radical Hospitality: Benedict's Way of Love* (Brewster, MA: Paraclete Press, 2002), 50.
2. Nhat Hanh, *Peace Is Every Step*, 53–55.
3. Ibid., 52.
4. Henri J. M. Nouwen, *Reaching Out: The Three Movements of the Spiritual Life*. (New York: Doubleday, 1986), 37–48.
5. Ibid., 30.
6. Henri J. M. Nouwen, "Moving from Solitude to Community to Ministry," *Leadership Journal* 16, no. 2 (Spring, 1995), 82.
7. Brennan Manning, *The Ragamuffin Gospel* (Sisters, OR: Multnomah Publishers, 2005), 27–28.
8. Kallistos Ware, interview, 64.
9. Matthew Fox, *Creativity* (New York: Jeremy P. Tarcher, 2004), 51.
10. Thomas Merton, cited in M. Basil Pennington, *True Self, False Self: Unmasking the Spirit Within* (New York: Crossroad, 2000), 89–90.
11. Ibid., 91.
12. "In God Alone," in *Songs & Prayers from Taizé* (Chicago: GIA Publications, 1991), 41.
13. Wayne Muller, *Sabbath: Finding Rest, Renewal, and Delight in Our Busy Lives* (New York: Bantam Books, 2000), 92.
14. Nouwen, "Moving from Solitude to Community to Ministry," 82–83.
15. This statement is attributed to the Indian holy man Swami Nityananda, to whom the temple is dedicated. The temple is located in South Fallsburg, New York.

CHAPTER THREE

1. The three A's—Awareness, Acceptance, Action—are used for spiritual growth in many 12-step programs.
2. Nouwen, *Reaching Out*, 81–82.

3. Suzuki, *Zen Mind, Beginner's Mind*, 32.
4. Christine Pohl, *Making Room: Recovering Hospitality as a Christian Tradition* (Grand Rapids, MI: Eerdmans, 1999), 102.

CHAPTER FOUR

1. Luke 10:25–37.
2. Jesus scholar Marcus Borg suggests that the Greek words usually translated as "eternal life" actually reflect a Jewish idea of "the life of the age to come." He also notes that when this phrase is used in John's Gospel, it is often spoken of in the present tense, suggesting that the "life of the age to come" has come already. The significance of Borg's work is that it shifts the theological emphasis from winning life in heaven after death to the idea of gaining a new way of life in this life. For a full discussion of this, see Marcus J. Borg, *The Heart of Christianity: Rediscovering a Life of Faith* (San Francisco: HarperSanFrancisco, 2003), 174.
3. The Trinity is traditionally referred to as Father, Son, and Holy Spirit, but is also referred to in many other ways. Creator, Redeemer, and Sustainer, is one common form.
4. Nhat Hanh, *Peace Is Every Step*, 95. He writes, "If you are a poet, you will clearly see that there is a cloud floating in this sheet of paper. Without a cloud, there will be no rain; without rain, the trees cannot grow; and without trees, we cannot make paper. The cloud is essential for the paper to exist. If the cloud is not here, the sheet of paper cannot be here either. So we can say that the cloud and the paper *inter-are*."
5. Acts 17:28, NRSV.
6. Suzuki, *Zen Mind, Beginner's Mind*, 119.
7. Thomas Merton, *Conjectures of a Guilty Bystander* (New York: Doubleday, 1989), 156.
8. Ibid., 157.
9. Ibid., 158.
10. Ibid.
11. Suzuki, *Zen Mind, Beginner's Mind*, 119.
12. *Hotel Rwanda*, movie, directed by Terry George (Kigali Releasing Limited, 2004).
13. Mother Teresa, *A Gift for God: Prayers and Meditations* (San Francisco: Harper & Row, 1975), 40.
14. Daniel Homan and Lonni Pratt, *Radical Hospitality: Benedict's Way of Love* (Brewster, MA: Paraclete Press, 2002), 41.

15. Sue Monk Kidd, *The Secret Life of Bees* (New York: Penguin, 2003), 82.

CHAPTER FIVE

1. Nouwen, *Reaching Out*, 106.
2. Ibid., 67.
3. Ibid., 65.
4. Cited in Swami Anantananda, *What's on My Mind? Becoming Inspired with New Perception* (South Fallsburg, NY: SYDA Foundation, 1996), 59.
5. Henepola Gunaratana, *Mindfulness in Plain English* (Boston: Wisdom Publications, 1992), 186.
6. Anantananda, *What's on My Mind?*, 57.
7. Ibid.
8. John Grimes, *A Concise Dictionary of Indian Philosophy: Sanskrit Terms Defined in English* (New York: State University of New York Press, 1989), 100.
9. Anantananda, *What's on My Mind?*, 60.
10. Pohl, *Making Room*, 148.
11. Martha Nussbaum, cited in ibid., 149.
12. Gunaratana, *Mindfulness in Plain English*, 48.
13. Ibid., 186.
14. Ibid., 185.
15. Ibid., 48.
16. Ibid., 49.
17. Anantananda, *What's on My Mind?*, 78.
18. Cheri Huber, *How to Get from Where You Are to Where You Want to Be* (Carlsbad, CA: Hay House, 2000), 84.
19. Ibid., 84–85.
20. I've actually encountered this story in association with different religious traditions. In some versions the seeker is a Christian, in others, a Jew. Sometimes there is a wise one, a rabbi, or God's own self escorting the seeker to the doors of heaven and hell to take a peek inside. This is my own rendition of the story.
21. Ana María Pineda, "Hospitality," in Dorothy C. Bass, ed., *Practicing Our Faith: A Way of Life for a Searching People* (San Francisco: Jossey-Bass, 1997), 33.
22. Nouwen, *Reaching Out*, 107.
23. Martin Luther King Jr., "Letter from Birmingham Jail," in *A Testament of Hope: The Essential Writings and Speeches of Martin*

Luther King Jr., ed. James M. Washington (San Francisco: Harper SanFrancisco, 1986), 290.

CHAPTER SIX

1. Martin Luther King Jr., *The Autobiography of Martin Luther King Jr.*, ed. Clayborne Carson (New York: Warner Books, 1998), 7.
2. "Soul Force," *Time*, March 30, 1931.
3. Mahatma Gandhi, *The Essential Gandhi: An Anthology of His Writings on His Life, Work, and Ideas*, ed. Louis Fischer (New York: Vintage Books, 2002), 174.
4. Ibid., xviii.
5. Ibid., 79.
6. "Soul Force," *Time*, 1931.
7. King, *The Autobiography of Martin Luther King Jr.*, 78.
8. Ibid., p. 77.
9. "Soul Force Wins," *Time*, October 3, 1932.
10. King, *The Autobiography of Martin Luther King Jr.*, 67.
11. Martin Luther King Jr., "Loving Your Enemies," in *A Knock at Midnight: Inspiration from the Great Sermons of Reverend Martin Luther King Jr.*, ed. Clayborne Carson and Peter Holloran (New York: Warner Books, 1998), 41–60.
12. Matthew 5:43–45, New Revised Standard Version.
13. King, "Loving Your Enemies," 42, 46, 47.
14. Ibid., 56–57.
15. Gandhi, *The Essential Gandhi*, 294.
16. King, "Loving Your Enemies," 57.
17. Ibid., 43–44.
18. Matthew 7:3, NRSV. King referenced a different translation. See King, "Loving Your Enemies," 45.
19. Ibid., 46.
20. Ibid.
21. Matthew 5:43–45.
22. Matthew 5:38–39, NRSV.
23. This is a paraphrase of a story found in Pema Chödrön, *The Wisdom of No Escape and the Path of Loving-Kindness* (Boston: Shambhala, 1991), 31.
24. Nelson Mandela, "The Sacred Warrior," *Time*, December 27, 1999.
25. King, *The Autobiography of Martin Luther King Jr.*, 68.

26. Gandhi, *The Essential Gandhi*, 281.
27. Ibid.
28. King, "Loving Your Enemies," 59.
29. Ibid., 53–54.

CHAPTER SEVEN

1. Fiona Bowie and Oliver Davies, eds., *Hildegard of Bingen: Mystical Writings* (New York: Crossroad, 1992), 28.
2. Bernard McGinn, *The Essential Writings of Christian Mysticism* (New York: Modern Library, 2006), 291.
3. Lao Tsu, *Tao Te Ching*, trans. Gia-Fu Feng and Jane English (New York: Vintage Books, 1989), 15.
4. Jacob Needleman, Introduction. *Tao Te Ching*, vi.
5. Ibid.
6. Matthew Fox, *Radical Prayer*, audio presentation (Boulder, CO: Sounds True, 2003), disc 2.
7. Cited in Jeffrey Schaire, "Georgia O'Keeffe in Love" in *Arts & Antiques*, September 1987, 62.
8. Sally McFague, *Super, Natural Christians: How We Should Love Nature* (Minneapolis: Fortress Press, 1997), 29.
9. Martin Buber, *I and Thou* (New York: Simon & Schuster, 1996), 67.
10. Ibid., 57–59.
11. Ibid., 56.
12. McFague, *Super, Natural Christians*, 31–32.
13. Lao Tsu, *Tao Te Ching*, 65.
14. Buber, *I and Thou*, 67.
15. Nouwen, *Reaching Out*, 107.
16. www.quakerearthcare.org/SpiritualityandEarthcare/greenwitness.htm
17. Henri J. M. Nouwen, *Clowning in Rome: Reflections on Solitude, Celibacy, Prayer, and Contemplation* (New York: Doubleday, 2000), 87–88.
18. Stephanie Spellers, *Radical Welcome: Embracing God, the Other, and the Spirit of Transformation* (New York: Church Publishing, 2006), 18.

SUGGESTIONS FOR FURTHER READING

Anantananda, Swami. *What's on My Mind? Becoming Inspired with New Perception*. South Fallsburg, NY: SYDA Foundation, 1996.

Armstrong, Karen. *A History of God: The 4,000 Year Quest of Judaism, Christianity and Islam*. New York: Ballantine Books, 1993.

Bass, Diana Butler. *Christianity for the Rest of Us: How the Neighborhood Church Is Transforming the Faith*. San Francisco: HarperSanFrancisco, 2006.

Bass, Dorothy C., ed. *Practicing Our Faith: A Way of Life for a Searching People*. San Francisco: Jossey-Bass, 1997.

Borg, Marcus J. *The Heart of Christianity: Rediscovering a Life of Faith*. San Francisco: HarperSanFrancisco, 2003.

Bowie, Fiona, and Oliver Davies, eds. *Hildegard of Bingen: Mystical Writings*. New York: Crossroad, 1992.

Buber, Martin. *I and Thou*. New York: Touchstone, 1996.

———. *The Way of Response*. New York: Schocken Books, 1966.

Chödrön, Pema. *The Wisdom of No Escape and the Path of Loving-Kindness*. Boston: Shambhala, 1991.

de Mello, Anthony. *Sadhana, A Way to God: Christian Exercises in Eastern Form*. New York: Image Books, 1984.

Eckhart, Meister. *Meister Eckhart: A Modern Translation*. Raymond Bernard Blakney, trans. New York: Harper & Row, 1941.

Ford, Marcia. *Finding Hope: Cultivating God's Gift of a Hopeful Spirit*. Woodstock, VT: SkyLight Paths Publishing, 2007.

———. *The Sacred Art of Forgiveness: Forgiving Ourselves and Others through God's Grace*. Woodstock, VT: SkyLight Paths Publishing, 2006.

Fox, Matthew. *Creativity: Where the Divine and the Human Meet*. New York: Jeremy P. Tarcher, 2004.

——, ed. *Hildegard of Bingen's Book of Divine Works: With Letters and Songs*. Santa Fe, NM: Bear & Company, 1987.

——. *Radical Prayer*. Audio Presentation. Boulder, CO: Sounds True, 2003.

Gandhi, Mahatma. *An Autobiography: The Story of My Experiments with Truth*. Boston: Beacon Press, 1993. First published 1957.

——. *The Essential Gandhi: An Anthology of His Writings on His Life, Work, and Ideas*, 2nd ed. Edited by Louis Fischer. New York: Vintage Books, 2002. First published 1983.

Grimes, John. *A Concise Dictionary of Indian Philosophy: Sanskrit Terms Defined in English*. New York: State University of New York Press, 1989.

Gunaratana, Venerable Henepola. *Mindfulness in Plain English*. Boston: Wisdom Publications, 1992.

Heschel, Abraham Joshua. *The Sabbath*. New York: Farrar, Straus and Giroux, 1951.

Hildegard of Bingen. *Symphonia: A Critical Edition of the Symphonia Armonie Celestium Revelationum*. Translated by Barbara Newman. Ithaca, NY: Cornell University Press, 1998.

Homan, Father Daniel, O.S.B, and Lonni Pratt. *Radical Hospitality: Benedict's Way of Love*. Brewster, MA: Paraclete Press, 2002.

Huber, Cheri. *How to Get from Where You Are to Where You Want to Be*. Carlsbad, CA: Hay House, 2000.

Keating, Thomas. *Foundations for Centering Prayer and the Christian Contemplative Life*. New York: Continuum, 2002.

Kedar, Karyn D. *The Bridge to Forgiveness: Stories and Prayers for Finding God and Restoring Wholeness*. Woodstock, VT: Jewish Lights Publishing, 2007.

Kidd, Sue Monk. *The Secret Life of Bees*. New York: Penguin, 2003.

King, Martin Luther, Jr. *The Autobiography of Martin Luther King Jr*. Edited by Clayborne Carson. New York: Warner Books, 1998.

——. *A Knock at Midnight: Inspiration from the Great Sermons of Reverend Martin Luther King Jr*. Edited by Clayborne Carson and Peter Holloran. New York: Warner Books, 1998.

——. *A Testament of Hope: The Essential Writings and Speeches of Martin Luther King Jr*. Edited by James M. Washington. San Francisco: Harper SanFrancisco, 1986.

Lin, Derek. *Tao Te Ching: Annotated & Explained.* Woodstock, VT: SkyLight Paths Publishing, 2006.

Manning, Brennan. *The Ragamuffin Gospel.* Sisters, OR: Multnomah Publishers, 2005. First published 1990.

Marshall, Jay. *Thanking & Blessing—The Sacred Art: Spiritual Vitality through Gratefulness.* Woodstock, VT: SkyLight Paths Publishing, 2007.

McFague, Sally. *Super, Natural Christians: How We Should Love Nature.* Minneapolis: Fortress Press, 1997.

McGee, Margaret D. *Sacred Attention: A Spiritual Practice for Finding God in the Moment.* Woodstock, VT: SkyLight Paths Publishing, 2007.

McGinn, Bernard. *The Essential Writings of Christian Mysticism.* New York: Modern Library, 2006.

Merton, Thomas. *Conjectures of a Guilty Bystander.* New York: Image Books, 1989. First published 1966.

Muller, Wayne. *Sabbath: Finding Rest, Renewal, and Delight in Our Busy Lives.* New York: Bantam Books, 2000. First published 1999.

Nhat Hanh, Thich. *Being Peace.* Berkeley: Parallax Press, 1987.

———. *Living Buddha, Living Christ.* New York: Riverhead Books, 1995.

———. *Peace Is Every Step: The Path of Mindfulness in Everyday Life.* New York: Bantam Books, 1991.

Nouwen, Henri J. M. *Clowning in Rome: Reflections on Solitude, Celibacy, Prayer, and Contemplation.* New York: Image Books, 2000. First published 1979.

———. *Reaching Out: The Three Movements of the Spiritual Life.* New York: Doubleday, 1986.

———. "Moving from Solitude to Community to Ministry." *Leadership Journal* 16, no. 2 (Spring, 1995).

Pennington, M. Basil. *True Self, False Self: Unmasking the Spirit Within.* New York: Crossroad, 2000.

Pennington, M. Basil, Thomas Keating, and Thomas E. Clarke. *Finding Grace at the Center: The Beginning of Centering Prayer.* Woodstock, VT: SkyLight Paths Publishing, 2002.

Pohl, Christine D. *Making Room: Recovering Hospitality as a Christian Tradition.* Grand Rapids, MI: Eerdmans, 1999.

Shapiro, Rami. *The Sacred Art of Lovingkindness: Preparing to Practice.* Woodstock, VT: SkyLight Paths Publishing, 2006.

Spellers, Stephanie. *Radical Welcome: Embracing God, the Other, and the Spirit of Transformation.* New York: Church Publishing, 2006.

Suzuki, Shunryu. *Zen Mind, Beginner's Mind: Informal Talks on Zen Meditation and Practice.* New York: Weatherhill, 1970.

Teresa, Mother. *A Gift for God: Prayers and Meditations.* San Francisco: Harper & Row, 1975.

Teutsch, David A. *Spiritual Community: The Power to Restore Hope, Commitment and Joy.* Woodstock, VT: Jewish Lights Publishing, 2005.

Tsu, Lao. *Tao Te Ching.* Gia-Fu Feng and Jane English, trans. New York: Vintage Books, 1989.

Ware, Kallistos. "An Interview with Bishop Kallistos Ware." By James Moran. *Parabola: The Magazine of Myth and Tradition.* Vol. X, No. 1, February 1985.

Wolfson, Ron. *The Spirituality of Welcoming: How to Transform Your Congregation into a Sacred Community.* Woodstock, VT: Jewish Lights Publishing, 2006.

Wolters, Clifton, trans. *The Cloud of Unknowing and Other Works.* London: Penguin Books, 1978. First published 1961.

INDEX OF EXERCISES AND PRACTICES

Practicing Receptivity through Centering Prayer   17

Receptivity, Reverence, and Generosity to God in Daily Life   20

Finding Your Inner Sanctuary   25

Thich Nhat Hanh's Five Steps for Transforming Feelings   37

Entering a Receptive, Reverent Space through Mantra Repetition   44

Generosity: Nurturing the Self   48

Apply Awareness to Develop Receptivity   55

Develop Acceptance to Foster Reverence   60

Hospitality Practices with Family   66

Invite People into Your Home on a Regular Basis   88

Generosity of Attention—Making Intentional Conversation   89

Escorting Yourself through Moments of Fear   101

Distinguishing Appropriate Boundaries: Trusting Your Intuition   105

Self-Examination   127

A Circle of Love: Draw It Large Enough
    to Include Your Adversary   131

Identify with Your Adversary   133

Replace Retaliatory Feelings with Love and Compassion   137

The City Is Creation, Too   145

Practice Seeing Creation with Reverence   153

Practice Simple Living as Embodiment
    of Hospitality to Creation   158

Children's Spirituality

Adam and Eve's First Sunset: God's New Day
by Sandy Eisenberg Sasso; Full-color illus. by Joani Keller Rothenberg
9 x 12, 32 pp, Full-color illus., HC, 978-1-58023-177-0 **$17.95** *For ages 4 & up (a Jewish Lights book)*

Because Nothing Looks Like God
by Lawrence and Karen Kushner; Full-color illus. by Dawn W. Majewski
Real-life examples of happiness and sadness introduce children to the possibilities of spiritual life. 11 x 8½, 32 pp, HC, Full-color illus., 978-1-58023-092-6 **$16.95**
For ages 4 & up (a Jewish Lights book)

Also available: **Teacher's Guide,** 8½ x 11, 22 pp, PB, 978-1-58023-140-4 **$6.95** *For ages 5–8*

Becoming Me: A Story of Creation
by Martin Boroson; Full-color illus. by Christopher Gilvan-Cartwright
Told in the personal "voice" of the Creator, a story about creation and relationship that is about each one of us.
8 x 10, 32 pp, Full-color illus., HC, 978-1-893361-11-9 **$16.95** *For ages 4 & up*

But God Remembered: Stories of Women from Creation to the Promised Land   by Sandy Eisenberg Sasso; Full-color illus. by Bethanne Andersen
A fascinating collection of four different stories of women only briefly mentioned in biblical tradition and religious texts. 9 x 12, 32 pp, HC, Full-color illus., 978-1-879045-43-9 **$16.95**
For ages 8 & up (a Jewish Lights book)

Cain & Abel: Finding the Fruits of Peace
by Sandy Eisenberg Sasso; Full-color illus. by Joani Keller Rothenberg
A sensitive recasting of the ancient tale shows we have the power to deal with anger in positive ways. "Editor's Choice"—American Library Association's *Booklist*
9 x 12, 32 pp, HC, Full-color illus., 978-1-58023-123-7 **$16.95** *For ages 5 & up (a Jewish Lights book)*

Does God Hear My Prayer?
by August Gold; Full-color photos by Diane Hardy Waller
Introduces preschoolers and young readers to prayer and how it helps them express their own emotions. 10 x 8½, 32 pp, Quality PB, Full-color photo illus., 978-1-59473-102-0 **$8.99**

The 11th Commandment: Wisdom from Our Children by The Children of America
"If there were an Eleventh Commandment, what would it be?" Children of many religious denominations across America answer this question—in their own drawings and words. "A rare book of spiritual celebration for all people, of all ages, for all time." —*Bookviews*
8 x 10, 48 pp, HC, Full-color illus., 978-1-879045-46-0 **$16.95** *For all ages (a Jewish Lights book)*

For Heaven's Sake   by Sandy Eisenberg Sasso; Full-color illus. by Kathryn Kunz Finney
Everyone talked about heaven: "Thank heavens." "Heaven forbid." "For heaven's sake, Isaiah." But no one would say what heaven was or how to find it. So Isaiah decides to find out, by seeking answers from many different people.
9 x 12, 32 pp, HC, Full-color illus., 978-1-58023-054-0 **$16.95** *For ages 4 & up (a Jewish Lights book)*

God in Between   by Sandy Eisenberg Sasso; Full-color illus. by Sally Sweetland
A magical, mythical tale that teaches that God can be found where we are.
9 x 12, 32 pp, HC, Full-color illus., 978-1-879045-86-6 **$16.95** *For ages 4 & up (a Jewish Lights book)*

God's Paintbrush: Special 10th Anniversary Edition
Invites children of all faiths and backgrounds to encounter God through moments in their own lives. 11 x 8½, 32 pp, Full-color illus., HC, 978-1-58023-195-4 **$17.95** *For ages 4 & up*

Also available: **God's Paintbrush Teacher's Guide** 8½ x 11, 32 pp, PB, 978-1-879045-57-6 **$8.95**

God's Paintbrush Celebration Kit
A Spiritual Activity Kit for Teachers and Students of All Faiths, All Backgrounds
Additional activity sheets available:
8-Student Activity Sheet Pack (40 sheets/5 sessions), 978-1-58023-058-2 **$19.95**
Single-Student Activity Sheet Pack (5 sessions), 978-1-58023-059-9 **$3.95**

Children's Spirituality

ENDORSED BY CATHOLIC, PROTESTANT, JEWISH, AND BUDDHIST RELIGIOUS LEADERS

Remembering My Grandparent: A Kid's Own Grief Workbook in the Christian Tradition *by Nechama Liss-Levinson, PhD, and Rev. Molly Phinney Baskette, MDiv*
8 x 10, 48 pp, 2-color text, HC, 978-1-59473-212-6 **$16.99** *For ages 7–13*

Does God Ever Sleep? *by Joan Sauro, CSJ; Full-color photos*
A charming nighttime reminder that God is always present in our lives.
10 x 8½, 32 pp, Quality PB, Full-color photos, 978-1-59473-110-5 **$8.99** *For ages 3–6*

Does God Forgive Me? *by August Gold; Full-color photos by Diane Hardy Waller*
Gently shows how God forgives all that we do if we are truly sorry.
10 x 8½, 32 pp, Quality PB, Full-color photos, 978-1-59473-142-6 **$8.99** *For ages 3–6*

God Said Amen *by Sandy Eisenberg Sasso; Full-color illus. by Avi Katz*
A warm and inspiring tale of two kingdoms that shows us that we need only reach out to each other to find the answers to our prayers.
9 x 12, 32 pp, HC, Full-color illus., 978-1-58023-080-3 **$16.95**
For ages 4 & up (a Jewish Lights book)

How Does God Listen? *by Kay Lindahl; Full-color photos by Cynthia Maloney*
How do we know when God is listening to us? Children will find the answers to these questions as they engage their senses while the story unfolds, learning how God listens in the wind, waves, clouds, hot chocolate, perfume, our tears and our laughter.
10 x 8½, 32 pp, Quality PB, Full-color photos, 978-1-59473-084-9 **$8.99** *For ages 3–6*

In God's Hands *by Lawrence Kushner and Gary Schmidt; Full-color illus. by Matthew J. Baeck*
9 x 12, 32 pp, Full-color illus., HC, 978-1-58023-224-1 **$16.99** *For ages 5 & up (a Jewish Lights book)*

In God's Name *by Sandy Eisenberg Sasso; Full-color illus. by Phoebe Stone*
Like an ancient myth in its poetic text and vibrant illustrations, this award-winning modern fable about the search for God's name celebrates the diversity and, at the same time, the unity of all the people of the world.
9 x 12, 32 pp, HC, Full-color illus., 978-1-879045-26-2 **$16.99**
For ages 4 & up (a Jewish Lights book)

Also available in Spanish: **El nombre de Dios**
9 x 12, 32 pp, HC, Full-color illus., 978-1-893361-63-8 **$16.95**

In Our Image: God's First Creatures
by Nancy Sohn Swartz; Full-color illus. by Melanie Hall
A playful new twist on the Genesis story—from the perspective of the animals. Celebrates the interconnectedness of nature and the harmony of all living things. 9 x 12, 32 pp, HC, Full-color illus., 978-1-879045-99-6 **$16.95**
For ages 4 & up (a Jewish Lights book)

Noah's Wife: The Story of Naamah
by Sandy Eisenberg Sasso; Full-color illus. by Bethanne Andersen
This new story, based on an ancient text, opens readers' religious imaginations to new ideas about the well-known story of the Flood. When God tells Noah to bring the animals of the world onto the ark, God also calls on Naamah, Noah's wife, to save each plant on Earth.
9 x 12, 32 pp, HC, Full-color illus., 978-1-58023-134-3 **$16.95**
For ages 4 & up (a Jewish Lights book)

Also available: **Naamah:** Noah's Wife (A Board Book)
by Sandy Eisenberg Sasso; Full-color illus. by Bethanne Andersen
5 x 5, 24 pp, Board Book, Full-color illus., 978-1-893361-56-0 **$7.99** *For ages 0–4*

Where Does God Live? *by August Gold and Matthew J. Perlman*
Using simple, everyday examples that children can relate to, this colorful book helps young readers develop a personal understanding of God.
10 x 8½, 32 pp, Quality PB, Full-color photo illus., 978-1-893361-39-3 **$8.99** *For ages 3–6*

Children's Spirituality—Board Books

Adam and Eve's New Day (A Board Book)
by Sandy Eisenberg Sasso; Full-color illus. by Joani Keller Rothenberg
A lesson in hope for every child who has worried about what comes next. Abridged from *Adam and Eve's First Sunset*.
5 x 5, 24 pp, Full-color illus., Board Book, 978-1-59473-205-8 **$7.99** *For ages 0–4*

How Did the Animals Help God? (A Board Book)
by Nancy Sohn Swartz; Full-color illus. by Melanie Hall
Abridged from *In Our Image*, God asks all of nature to offer gifts to humankind—with a promise that they will care for creation in return.
5 x 5, 24 pp, Board Book, Full-color illus., 978-1-59473-044-3 **$7.99** *For ages 0–4*

Where Is God? (A Board Book)
by Lawrence and Karen Kushner; Full-color illus. by Dawn W. Majewski A gentle way for young children to explore how God is with us every day, in every way. Abridged from *Because Nothing Looks Like God.*
5 x 5, 24 pp, Board Book, Full-color illus., 978-1-893361-17-1 **$7.99** *For ages 0–4*

What Does God Look Like? (A Board Book)
by Lawrence and Karen Kushner; Full-color illus. by Dawn W. Majewski
A simple way for young children to explore the ways that we "see" God. Abridged from *Because Nothing Looks Like God.*
5 x 5, 24 pp, Board Book, Full-color illus., 978-1-893361-23-2 **$7.95** *For ages 0–4*

How Does God Make Things Happen? (A Board Book)
by Lawrence and Karen Kushner; Full-color illus. by Dawn W. Majewski
A charming invitation for young children to explore how God makes things happen in our world. Abridged from *Because Nothing Looks Like God.*
5 x 5, 24 pp, Board Book, Full-color illus., 978-1-893361-24-9 **$7.95** *For ages 0–4*

What Is God's Name? (A Board Book)
by Sandy Eisenberg Sasso; Full-color illus. by Phoebe Stone
Everyone and everything in the world has a name. What is God's name? Abridged from the award-winning *In God's Name.*
5 x 5, 24 pp, Board Book, Full-color illus., 978-1-893361-10-2 **$7.99** *For ages 0–4*

What You Will See Inside ...

This important new series of books, each with many full-color photos, is designed to show children ages 6 and up the Who, What, When, Where, Why and How of traditional houses of worship, liturgical celebrations, and rituals of different world faiths, empowering them to respect and understand their own religious traditions—and those of their friends and neighbors.

What You Will See Inside a Catholic Church
by Reverend Michael Keane; Foreword by Robert J. Keeley, EdD
Full-color photos by Aaron Pepis
8½ x 10½, 32 pp, Full-color photos, HC, 978-1-893361-54-6 **$17.95**
Also available in Spanish: **Lo que se puede ver dentro de una iglesia católica**
8½ x 10½, 32 pp, Full-color photos, HC, 978-1-893361-66-9 **$16.95**

What You Will See Inside a Hindu Temple
by Dr. Mahendra Jani and Dr. Vandana Jani; Full-color photos by Neirah Bhargava and Vijay Dave
8½ x 10½, 32 pp, Full-color photos, HC, 978-1-59473-116-7 **$17.99**

What You Will See Inside a Mosque
by Aisha Karen Khan; Full-color photos by Aaron Pepis
8½ x 10½, 32 pp, Full-color photos, HC, 978-1-893361-60-7 **$16.95**

What You Will See Inside a Synagogue
by Rabbi Lawrence A. Hoffman and Dr. Ron Wolfson; Full-color photos by Bill Aron
8½ x 10½, 32 pp, Full-color photos, HC, 978-1-59473-012-2 **$17.99**

Children's Spiritual Biography

Ten Amazing People
And How They Changed the World
by *Maura D. Shaw; Foreword by Dr. Robert Coles*
Full-color illus. by Stephen Marchesi

For ages
7 & up

Black Elk • Dorothy Day • Malcolm X • Mahatma Gandhi • Martin Luther King, Jr. • Mother Teresa • Janusz Korczak • Desmond Tutu • Thich Nhat Hanh • Albert Schweitzer

This vivid, inspirational and authoritative book will open new possibilities for children by telling the stories of how ten of the past century's greatest leaders changed the world in important ways.

8½ x 11, 48 pp, HC, Full-color illus., 978-1-893361-47-8 **$17.95**
For ages 7 & up

Spiritual Biographies for Young People—For ages 7 and up

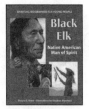   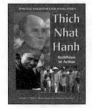

Black Elk: Native American Man of Spirit
by Maura D. Shaw; Full-color illus. by Stephen Marchesi
Through historically accurate illustrations and photos, inspiring age-appropriate activities and Black Elk's own words, this colorful biography introduces children to a remarkable person who ensured that the traditions and beliefs of his people would not be forgotten.
6¾ x 8¾, 32 pp, HC, Full-color and b/w illus., 978-1-59473-043-6 **$12.99**

Dorothy Day: A Catholic Life of Action
by Maura D. Shaw; Full-color illus. by Stephen Marchesi
Introduces children to one of the most inspiring women of the twentieth century, a down-to-earth spiritual leader who saw the presence of God in every person she met. Includes practical activities, a timeline and a list of important words to know.
6¾ x 8¾, 32 pp, HC, Full-color illus., 978-1-59473-011-5 **$12.99**

Gandhi: India's Great Soul
by Maura D. Shaw; Full-color illus. by Stephen Marchesi
There are a number of biographies of Gandhi written for young readers, but this is the only one that balances a simple text with illustrations, photographs, and activities that encourage children and adults to talk about how to make changes happen without violence. Introduces children to important concepts of freedom, equality and justice among people of all backgrounds and religions.
6¾ x 8¾, 32 pp, HC, Full-color illus., 978-1-893361-91-1 **$12.95**

Thich Nhat Hanh: Buddhism in Action
by Maura D. Shaw; Full-color illus. by Stephen Marchesi
Warm illustrations, photos, age-appropriate activities and Thich Nhat Hanh's own poems introduce a great man to children in a way they can understand and enjoy. Includes a list of important Buddhist words to know.
6¾ x 8¾, 32 pp, HC, Full-color illus., 978-1-893361-87-4 **$12.95**

Kabbalah from Jewish Lights Publishing

Awakening to Kabbalah: The Guiding Light of Spiritual Fulfillment
by Rav Michael Laitman, PhD 6 x 9, 192 pp, HC, 978-1-58023-264-7 **$21.99**

Cast in God's Image: Discover Your Personality Type Using the Enneagram and Kabbalah
by Rabbi Howard A. Addison 7 x 9, 176 pp, Quality PB, 978-1-58023-124-4 **$16.95**

Ehyeh: A Kabbalah for Tomorrow *by Dr. Arthur Green*
6 x 9, 224 pp, Quality PB, 978-1-58023-213-5 **$16.99**

The Enneagram and Kabbalah, 2nd Edition: Reading Your Soul
by Rabbi Howard A. Addison 6 x 9, 192 pp, Quality PB, 978-1-58023-229-6 **$16.99**

Finding Joy: A Practical Spiritual Guide to Happiness *by Dannel I. Schwartz with Mark Hass*
6 x 9, 192 pp, Quality PB, 978-1-58023-009-4 **$14.95**

The Gift of Kabbalah: Discovering the Secrets of Heaven, Renewing Your Life on Earth
by Tamar Frankiel, PhD 6 x 9, 256 pp, Quality PB, 978-1-58023-141-1 **$16.95**
HC, 978-1-58023-108-4 **$21.95**

Honey from the Rock: An Easy Introduction to Jewish Mysticism
by Lawrence Kushner 6 x 9, 176 pp, Quality PB, 978-1-58023-073-5 **$16.95**

Kabbalah: A Brief Introduction for Christians
by Tamar Frankiel, PhD 5½ x 8½, 176 pp, Quality PB, 978-1-58023-303-3 **$16.99**

Zohar: Annotated & Explained *Translation and Annotation by Dr. Daniel C. Matt*
Foreword by Andrew Harvey 5½ x 8¼, 176 pp, Quality PB, 978-1-893361-51-5 **$15.99**

Judaism / Christianity

Christians and Jews in Dialogue: Learning in the Presence of the Other
by Mary C. Boys and Sara S. Lee; Foreword by Dorothy C. Bass
Inspires renewed commitment to dialogue between religious traditions and illuminates how it should happen. Explains the transformative work of creating environments for Jews and Christians to study together and enter the dynamism of the other's religious tradition.
6 x 9, 240 pp, HC, 978-1-59473-144-0 **$21.99**

Healing the Jewish-Christian Rift: Growing Beyond Our Wounded History
by Ron Miller and Laura Bernstein; Foreword by Dr. Beatrice Bruteau
6 x 9, 288 pp, Quality PB, 978-1-59473-139-6 **$18.99**

Introducing My Faith and My Community
The Jewish Outreach Institute Guide for the Christian in a Jewish Interfaith Relationship
by Rabbi Kerry M. Olitzky 6 x 9, 176 pp, Quality PB, 978-1-58023-192-3 **$16.99** *(a Jewish Lights book)*

The Jewish Approach to God: A Brief Introduction for Christians
by Rabbi Neil Gillman 5½ x 8½, 192 pp, Quality PB, 978-1-58023-190-9 **$16.95** *(a Jewish Lights book)*

Jewish Holidays: A Brief Introduction for Christians
by Rabbi Kerry M. Olitzky and Rabbi Daniel Judson
5½ x 8½, 176 pp, Quality PB, 978-1-58023-302-6 **$16.99** *(a Jewish Lights book)*

Jewish Ritual: A Brief Introduction for Christians
by Rabbi Kerry M. Olitzky and Rabbi Daniel Judson
5½ x 8½, 144 pp, Quality PB, 978-1-58023-210-4 **$14.99** *(a Jewish Lights book)*

Jewish Spirituality: A Brief Introduction for Christians
by Rabbi Lawrence Kushner
5½ x 8½, 112 pp, Quality PB, 978-1-58023-150-3 **$12.95** *(a Jewish Lights book)*

A Jewish Understanding of the New Testament
by Rabbi Samuel Sandmel; new Preface by Rabbi David Sandmel
5½ x 8½, 368 pp, Quality PB, 978-1-59473-048-1 **$19.99**

We Jews and Jesus
Exploring Theological Differences for Mutual Understanding
by Rabbi Samuel Sandmel; new Preface by Rabbi David Sandmel A Classic Reprint
Written in a non-technical way for the layperson, this candid and forthright look at the what and why of the Jewish attitude toward Jesus is a clear and forceful exposition that guides both Christians and Jews in relevant discussion.
6 x 9, 192 pp, Quality PB, 978-1-59473-208-9 **$16.99**

Midrash Fiction / Folktales

Abraham's Bind & Other Bible Tales of Trickery, Folly, Mercy and Love by Michael J. Caduto

New retellings of episodes in the lives of familiar biblical characters explore relevant life lessons.

6 x 9, 224 pp, HC, 978-1-59473-186-0 **$19.99**

Daughters of the Desert: Stories of Remarkable Women from Christian, Jewish and Muslim Traditions by Claire Rudolf Murphy, Meghan Nuttall Sayres, Mary Cronk Farrell, Sarah Conover and Betsy Wharton

Breathes new life into the old tales of our female ancestors in faith. Uses traditional scriptural passages as starting points, then with vivid detail fills in historical context and place. Chapters reveal the voices of Sarah, Hagar, Huldah, Esther, Salome, Mary Magdalene, Lydia, Khadija, Fatima and many more. Historical fiction ideal for readers of all ages. Quality paperback includes reader's discussion guide.

5½ x 8½, 192 pp, Quality PB, 978-1-59473-106-8 **$14.99**
HC, 192 pp, 978-1-893361-72-0 **$19.95**

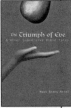

The Triumph of Eve & Other Subversive Bible Tales
by Matt Biers-Ariel

Many people were taught and remember only a one-dimensional Bible. These engaging retellings are the antidote to this—they're witty, often hilarious, always profound, and invite you to grapple with questions and issues that are often hidden in the original text.

5½ x 8½, 192 pp, Quality PB, 978-1-59473-176-1 **$14.99**
HC, 192 pp, 978-1-59473-040-5 **$19.99**

Also avail.: **The Triumph of Eve Teacher's Guide**
8½ x 11, 44 pp, PB, 978-1-59473-152-5 **$8.99**

Wisdom in the Telling
Finding Inspiration and Grace in Traditional Folktales and Myths Retold
by Lorraine Hartin-Gelardi
6 x 9, 224 pp, HC, 978-1-59473-185-3 **$19.99**

Religious Etiquette / Reference

How to Be a Perfect Stranger, 4th Edition: The Essential Religious Etiquette Handbook Edited by Stuart M. Matlins and Arthur J. Magida

The indispensable guidebook to help the well-meaning guest when visiting other people's religious ceremonies. A straightforward guide to the rituals and celebrations of the major religions and denominations in the United States and Canada from the perspective of an interested guest of any other faith, based on information obtained from authorities of each religion. Belongs in every living room, library and office. Covers:

African American Methodist Churches • Assemblies of God • Bahá'í • Baptist • Buddhist • Christian Church (Disciples of Christ) • Christian Science (Church of Christ, Scientist) • Churches of Christ • Episcopalian and Anglican • Hindu • Islam • Jehovah's Witnesses • Jewish • Lutheran • Mennonite/Amish • Methodist • Mormon (Church of Jesus Christ of Latter-day Saints) • Native American/First Nations • Orthodox Churches • Pentecostal Church of God • Presbyterian • Quaker (Religious Society of Friends) • Reformed Church in America/Canada • Roman Catholic • Seventh-day Adventist • Sikh • Unitarian Universalist • United Church of Canada • United Church of Christ

6 x 9, 432 pp, Quality PB, 978-1-59473-140-2 **$19.99**

The Perfect Stranger's Guide to Funerals and Grieving Practices: A Guide to Etiquette in Other People's Religious Ceremonies Edited by Stuart M. Matlins
6 x 9, 240 pp, Quality PB, 978-1-893361-20-1 **$16.95**

The Perfect Stranger's Guide to Wedding Ceremonies: A Guide to Etiquette in Other People's Religious Ceremonies Edited by Stuart M. Matlins
6 x 9, 208 pp, Quality PB, 978-1-893361-19-5 **$16.95**

Spiritual Biography—SkyLight Lives

SkyLight Lives reintroduces the lives and works of key spiritual figures of our time—people who by their teaching or example have challenged our assumptions about spirituality and have caused us to look at it in new ways.

The Life of Evelyn Underhill
An Intimate Portrait of the Groundbreaking Author of *Mysticism*
by Margaret Cropper; Foreword by Dana Greene
Evelyn Underhill was a passionate writer and teacher who wrote elegantly on mysticism, worship, and devotional life.
6 x 9, 288 pp, 5 b/w photos, Quality PB, 978-1-893361-70-6 **$18.95**

Mahatma Gandhi: His Life and Ideas
by Charles F. Andrews; Foreword by Dr. Arun Gandhi
Examines from a contemporary Christian activist's point of view the religious ideas and political dynamics that influenced the birth of the peaceful resistance movement.
6 x 9, 336 pp, 5 b/w photos, Quality PB, 978-1-893361-89-8 **$18.95**

Simone Weil: A Modern Pilgrimage
by Robert Coles
The extraordinary life of the spiritual philosopher who's been called both saint and madwoman.
6 x 9, 208 pp, Quality PB, 978-1-893361-34-8 **$16.95**

Zen Effects: The Life of Alan Watts
by Monica Furlong
Through his widely popular books and lectures, Alan Watts (1915–1973) did more to introduce Eastern philosophy and religion to Western minds than any figure before or since.
6 x 9, 264 pp, Quality PB, 978-1-893361-32-4 **$16.95**

More Spiritual Biography

Bede Griffiths: An Introduction to His Interspiritual Thought
by Wayne Teasdale
The first study of his contemplative experience and thought, exploring the intersection of Hinduism and Christianity.
6 x 9, 288 pp, Quality PB, 978-1-893361-77-5 **$18.95**

The Soul of the Story: Meetings with Remarkable People
by Rabbi David Zeller
Inspiring and entertaining, this compelling collection of spiritual adventures assures us that no spiritual lesson truly learned is ever lost.
6 x 9, 288 pp, HC, 978-1-58023-272-2 **$21.99** *(a Jewish Lights book)*

Spiritual Poetry—The Mystic Poets

Experience these mystic poets as you never have before. Each beautiful, compact book includes: a brief introduction to the poet's time and place; a summary of the major themes of the poet's mysticism and religious tradition; essential selections from the poet's most important works; and an appreciative preface by a contemporary spiritual writer.

   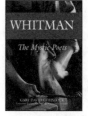

Hafiz: The Mystic Poets
Preface by Ibrahim Gamard
Hafiz is known throughout the world as Persia's greatest poet, with sales of his poems in Iran today only surpassed by those of the Qur'an itself. His probing and joyful verse speaks to people from all backgrounds who long to taste and feel divine love and experience harmony with all living things.
5 x 7¼, 144 pp, HC, 978-1-59473-009-2 **$16.99**

Hopkins: The Mystic Poets
Preface by Rev. Thomas Ryan, CSP
Gerard Manley Hopkins, Christian mystical poet, is beloved for his use of fresh language and startling metaphors to describe the world around him. Although his verse is lovely, beneath the surface lies a searching soul, wrestling with and yearning for God.
5 x 7¼, 112 pp, HC, 978-1-59473-010-8 **$16.99**

Tagore: The Mystic Poets
Preface by Swami Adiswarananda
Rabindranath Tagore is often considered the "Shakespeare" of modern India. A great mystic, Tagore was the teacher of W. B. Yeats and Robert Frost, the close friend of Albert Einstein and Mahatma Gandhi, and the winner of the Nobel Prize for Literature. This beautiful sampling of Tagore's two most important works, *The Gardener* and *Gitanjali,* offers a glimpse into his spiritual vision that has inspired people around the world.
5 x 7¼, 144 pp, HC, 978-1-59473-008-5 **$16.99**

Whitman: The Mystic Poets
Preface by Gary David Comstock
Walt Whitman was the most innovative and influential poet of the nineteenth century. This beautiful sampling of Whitman's most important poetry from *Leaves of Grass,* and selections from his prose writings, offers a glimpse into the spiritual side of his most radical themes—love for country, love for others, and love of Self.
5 x 7¼, 192 pp, HC, 978-1-59473-041-2 **$16.99**

Sacred Texts—SkyLight Illuminations Series

Offers today's spiritual seeker an accessible entry into the great classic texts of the world's spiritual traditions. Each classic is presented in an accessible translation, with facing pages of guided commentary from experts, giving you the keys you need to understand the history, context and meaning of the text. This series enables you, whatever your background, to experience and understand classic spiritual texts directly, and to make them a part of your life.

CHRISTIANITY

The End of Days: Essential Selections from Apocalyptic Texts— Annotated & Explained *Annotation by Robert G. Clouse*
Helps you understand the complex Christian visions of the end of the world.
5½ x 8½, 224 pp, Quality PB, 978-1-59473-170-9 **$16.99**

The Hidden Gospel of Matthew: Annotated & Explained
Translation & Annotation by Ron Miller
Takes you deep into the text cherished around the world to discover the words and events that have the strongest connection to the historical Jesus.
5½ x 8½, 272 pp, Quality PB, 978-1-59473-038-2 **$16.99**

The Lost Sayings of Jesus: Teachings from Ancient Christian, Jewish, Gnostic and Islamic Sources—Annotated & Explained
Translation & Annotation by Andrew Phillip Smith; Foreword by Stephan A. Hoeller
This collection of more than three hundred sayings depicts Jesus as a Wisdom teacher who speaks to people of all faiths as a mystic and spiritual master.
5½ x 8½, 240 pp, Quality PB, 978-1-59473-172-3 **$16.99**

Philokalia: The Eastern Christian Spiritual Texts—Selections Annotated & Explained *Annotation by Allyne Smith; Translation by G. E. H. Palmer, Phillip Sherrard and Bishop Kallistos Ware*
The first approachable introduction to the wisdom of the Philokalia, which is the classic text of Eastern Christian spirituality.
5½ x 8½, 240 pp, Quality PB, 978-1-59473-103-7 **$16.99**

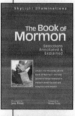

Spiritual Writings on Mary: Annotated & Explained
Annotation by Mary Ford-Grabowsky; Foreword by Andrew Harvey
Examines the role of Mary, the mother of Jesus, as a source of inspiration in history and in life today. 5½ x 8½, 288 pp, Quality PB, 978-1-59473-001-6 **$16.99**

The Way of a Pilgrim: The Jesus Prayer Journey—Annotated & Explained
Translation & Annotation by Gleb Pokrovsky; Foreword by Andrew Harvey
This classic of Russian spirituality is the delightful account of one man who sets out to learn the prayer of the heart, also known as the "Jesus prayer."
5½ x 8½, 160 pp, Illus., Quality PB, 978-1-893361-31-7 **$14.95**

MORMONISM

The Book of Mormon: Selections Annotated & Explained
Annotation by Jana Riess; Foreword by Phyllis Tickle
Explores the sacred epic that is cherished by more than twelve million members of the LDS church as the keystone of their faith.
5½ x 8½ , 272 pp, Quality PB, 978-1-59473-076-4 **$16.99**

NATIVE AMERICAN

Native American Stories of the Sacred: Annotated & Explained
Retold & Annotated by Evan T. Pritchard
Intended for more than entertainment, these teaching tales contain elegantly simple illustrations of time-honored truths.
5½ x 8½, 272 pp, Quality PB, 978-1-59473-112-9 **$16.99**

Sacred Texts—cont.

GNOSTICISM

The Gospel of Philip: Annotated & Explained
Translation & Annotation by Andrew Phillip Smith; Foreword by Stevan Davies
Reveals otherwise unrecorded sayings of Jesus and fragments of Gnostic mythology.
5½ x 8½, 160 pp, Quality PB, 978-1-59473-111-2 **$16.99**

The Gospel of Thomas: Annotated & Explained
Translation & Annotation by Stevan Davies Sheds new light on the origins of Christianity and
portrays Jesus as a wisdom-loving sage. 5½ x 8½, 192 pp, Quality PB, 978-1-893361-45-4 **$16.99**

The Secret Book of John: The Gnostic Gospel—Annotated & Explained
Translation & Annotation by Stevan Davies The most significant and influential text of
the ancient Gnostic religion. 5½ x 8½, 208 pp, Quality PB, 978-1-59473-082-5 **$16.99**

JUDAISM

The Divine Feminine in Biblical Wisdom Literature
Selections Annotated & Explained
Translation & Annotation by Rabbi Rami Shapiro; Foreword by Rev. Cynthia Bourgeault, PhD
Uses the Hebrew books of Psalms, Proverbs, Song of Songs, Ecclesiastes and Job,
Wisdom literature and the Wisdom of Solomon to clarify who Wisdom is.
5½ x 8½, 240 pp, Quality PB, 978-1-59473-109-9 **$16.99**

Ethics of the Sages: *Pirke Avot*—Annotated & Explained
Translation & Annotation by Rabbi Rami Shapiro Clarifies the ethical teachings of the
early Rabbis. 5½ x 8½, 192 pp, Quality PB, 978-1-59473-207-2 **$16.99**

Hasidic Tales: Annotated & Explained
Translation & Annotation by Rabbi Rami Shapiro
Introduces the legendary tales of the impassioned Hasidic rabbis, presenting them as
stories rather than as parables. 5½ x 8½, 240 pp, Quality PB, 978-1-893361-86-7 **$16.95**

The Hebrew Prophets: Selections Annotated & Explained
Translation & Annotation by Rabbi Rami Shapiro; Foreword by Zalman M. Schachter-Shalomi
Focuses on the central themes covered by all the Hebrew prophets.
5½ x 8½, 224 pp, Quality PB, 978-1-59473-037-5 **$16.99**

Zohar: Annotated & Explained *Translation & Annotation by Daniel C. Matt*
The best-selling author of *The Essential Kabbalah* brings together in one place the most
important teachings of the Zohar, the canonical text of Jewish mystical tradition.
5½ x 8½, 176 pp, Quality PB, 978-1-893361-51-5 **$15.99**

EASTERN RELIGIONS

Bhagavad Gita: Annotated & Explained *Translation by Shri Purohit Swami
Annotation by Kendra Crossen Burroughs* Explains references and philosophical terms,
shares the interpretations of famous spiritual leaders and scholars, and more.
5½ x 8½, 192 pp, Quality PB, 978-1-893361-28-7 **$16.95**

Dhammapada: Annotated & Explained *Translation by Max Müller and revised by
Jack Maguire; Annotation by Jack Maguire* Contains all of Buddhism's key teachings.
5½ x 8½, 160 pp, b/w photos, Quality PB, 978-1-893361-42-3 **$14.95**

Rumi and Islam: Selections from His Stories, Poems, and Discourses—
Annotated & Explained *Translation & Annotation by Ibrahim Gamard*
Focuses on Rumi's place within the Sufi tradition of Islam, providing insight into
the mystical side of the religion. 5½ x 8½, 240 pp, Quality PB, 978-1-59473-002-3 **$15.99**

Selections from the Gospel of Sri Ramakrishna: Annotated & Explained
Translation by Swami Nikhilananda; Annotation by Kendra Crossen Burroughs
Introduces the fascinating world of the Indian mystic and the universal appeal
of his message. 5½ x 8½, 240 pp, b/w photos, Quality PB, 978-1-893361-46-1 **$16.95**

Tao Te Ching: Annotated & Explained *Translation & Annotation by Derek Lin
Foreword by Lama Surya Das* Introduces an Eastern classic in an accessible, poetic
and completely original way. 5½ x 8½, 192 pp, Quality PB, 978-1-59473-204-1 **$16.99**

Spirituality

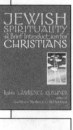

Jewish Spirituality: A Brief Introduction for Christians *by Lawrence Kushner*
5½ x 8½, 112 pp, Quality PB, 978-1-58023-150-3 **$12.95** *(a Jewish Lights book)*

Journeys of Simplicity: Traveling Light with Thomas Merton, Bashō, Edward Abbey,
Annie Dillard & Others *by Philip Harnden* 5 x 7¼, 144 pp, Quality PB, 978-1-59473-181-5 **$12.99**
128 pp, HC, 978-1-893361-76-8 **$16.95**

Keeping Spiritual Balance As We Grow Older: More than 65 Creative Ways to
Use Purpose, Prayer, and the Power of Spirit to Build a Meaningful Retirement
by Molly and Bernie Srode 8 x 8, 224 pp, Quality PB, 978-1-59473-042-9 **$16.99**

The Monks of Mount Athos: A Western Monk's Extraordinary Spiritual Journey on
Eastern Holy Ground *by M. Basil Pennington, ocso; Foreword by Archimandrite Dionysios*
6 x 9, 256 pp, 10+ b/w line drawings, Quality PB, 978-1-893361-78-2 **$18.95**

One God Clapping: The Spiritual Path of a Zen Rabbi *by Alan Lew with Sherrill Jaffe*
5½ x 8½, 336 pp, Quality PB, 978-1-58023-115-2 **$16.95** *(a Jewish Lights book)*

Prayer for People Who Think Too Much: A Guide to Everyday, Anywhere Prayer
from the World's Faith Traditions *by Mitch Finley*
5½ x 8½, 224 pp, Quality PB, 978-1-893361-21-8 **$16.99**; HC, 978-1-893361-00-3 **$21.95**

Show Me Your Way: The Complete Guide to Exploring Interfaith Spiritual Direction
by Howard A. Addison 5½ x 8½, 240 pp, Quality PB, 978-1-893361-41-6 **$16.95**

Spirituality 101: The Indispensable Guide to Keeping—or Finding—Your Spiritual Life
on Campus *by Harriet L. Schwartz, with contributions from college students at nearly thirty
campuses across the United States* 6 x 9, 272 pp, Quality PB, 978-1-59473-000-9 **$16.99**

Spiritually Incorrect: Finding God in All the *Wrong* Places *by Dan Wakefield; Illus. by
Marian DelVecchio* 5½ x 8½, 192 pp, b/w illus., Quality PB, 978-1-59473-137-2 **$15.99**

Spiritual Manifestos: Visions for Renewed Religious Life in America from Young
Spiritual Leaders of Many Faiths *Edited by Niles Elliot Goldstein; Preface by Martin E. Marty*
6 x 9, 256 pp, HC, 978-1-893361-09-6 **$21.95**

A Walk with Four Spiritual Guides: Krishna, Buddha, Jesus, and Ramakrishna
by Andrew Harvey 5½ x 8½, 192 pp, 10 b/w photos & illus.,Quality PB, 978-1-59473-138-9 **$15.99**

What Matters: Spiritual Nourishment for Head and Heart
by Frederick Franck 5 x 7¼, 128 pp, 50+ b/w illus., HC, 978-1-59473-013-9 **$16.99**

Who Is My God?, 2nd Edition: An Innovative Guide to Finding Your Spiritual Identity
Created by the Editors at SkyLight Paths 6 x 9, 160 pp, Quality PB, 978-1-59473-014-6 **$15.99**

Spirituality—A Week Inside

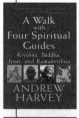

Come and Sit: A Week Inside Meditation Centers
by Marcia Z. Nelson; Foreword by Wayne Teasdale
The insider's guide to meditation in a variety of different spiritual traditions—
Buddhist, Hindu, Christian, Jewish, and Sufi traditions.
6 x 9, 224 pp, b/w photos, Quality PB, 978-1-893361-35-5 **$16.95**

Lighting the Lamp of Wisdom: A Week Inside a Yoga Ashram
by John Ittner; Foreword by Dr. David Frawley
This insider's guide to Hindu spiritual life takes you into a typical week of retreat
inside a yoga ashram to demystify the experience and show you what to expect.
6 x 9, 192 pp, 10+ b/w photos, Quality PB, 978-1-893361-52-2 **$15.95**

Making a Heart for God: A Week Inside a Catholic Monastery
by Dianne Aprile; Foreword by Brother Patrick Hart, ocso
Takes you to the Abbey of Gethsemani—the Trappist monastery in Kentucky
that was home to author Thomas Merton—to explore the details.
6 x 9, 224 pp, b/w photos, Quality PB, 978-1-893361-49-2 **$16.95**

Waking Up: A Week Inside a Zen Monastery
by Jack Maguire; Foreword by John Daido Loori, Roshi
An essential guide to what it's like to spend a week inside a Zen Buddhist monastery.
6 x 9, 224 pp, b/w photos, Quality PB, 978-1-893361-55-3 **$16.95**
HC, 978-1-893361-13-3 **$21.95**

Meditation / Prayer

Prayers to an Evolutionary God
by William Cleary; Afterword by Diarmuid O'Murchu
How is it possible to pray when God is dislocated from heaven, dispersed all around us, and more of a creative force than an all-knowing father? Inspired by the spiritual and scientific teachings of Diarmuid O'Murchu and Teilhard de Chardin, Cleary reveals that religion and science can be combined to create an expanding view of the universe—an evolutionary faith.
6 x 9, 208 pp, HC, 978-1-59473-006-1 **$21.99**

Psalms: A Spiritual Commentary
by M. Basil Pennington, OCSO; Illustrations by Phillip Ratner
Showing how the Psalms give profound and candid expression to both our highest aspirations and our deepest pain, the late, highly respected Cistercian Abbot M. Basil Pennington shares his reflections on some of the most beloved passages from the Bible's most widely read book.
6 x 9, 176 pp, HC, 24 full-page b/w illus., 978-1-59473-141-9 **$19.99**

The Song of Songs: A Spiritual Commentary
by M. Basil Pennington, OCSO; Illustrations by Phillip Ratner
Join the late M. Basil Pennington as he ruminates on the Bible's most challenging mystical text. Follow a path into the Songs that weaves through his inspired words and the evocative drawings of Jewish artist Phillip Ratner—a path that reveals your own humanity and leads to the deepest delight of your soul.
6 x 9, 160 pp, HC, 14 b/w illus., 978-1-59473-004-7 **$19.99**

Women of Color Pray: Voices of Strength, Faith, Healing, Hope and Courage
Edited and with Introductions by Christal M. Jackson
Through these prayers, poetry, lyrics, meditations and affirmations, you will share in the strong and undeniable connection women of color share with God. It will challenge you to explore new ways of prayerful expression.
5 x 7¼, 208 pp, Quality PB, 978-1-59473-077-1 **$15.99**

The Art of Public Prayer: Not for Clergy Only
by Lawrence A. Hoffman
An ecumenical resource for all people looking to change hardened worship patterns.
6 x 9, 288 pp, Quality PB, 978-1-893361-06-5 **$18.99**

Finding Grace at the Center, 3rd Ed.: The Beginning of Centering Prayer
by M. Basil Pennington, OCSO, Thomas Keating, OCSO, and Thomas E. Clarke, SJ
Foreword by Rev. Cynthia Bourgeault, PhD
5 x 7¼, 128 pp, Quality PB, 978-1-59473-182-2 **$12.99**

A Heart of Stillness: A Complete Guide to Learning the Art of Meditation
by David A. Cooper 5½ x 8½, 272 pp, Quality PB, 978-1-893361-03-4 **$16.95**

Meditation without Gurus: A Guide to the Heart of Practice
by Clark Strand 5½ x 8½, 192 pp, Quality PB, 978-1-893361-93-5 **$16.95**

Praying with Our Hands: 21 Practices of Embodied Prayer from the World's Spiritual Traditions
by Jon M. Sweeney; Photographs by Jennifer J. Wilson; Foreword by Mother Tessa Bielecki; Afterword by Taitetsu Unno, PhD
8 x 8, 96 pp, 22 duotone photos, Quality PB, 978-1-893361-16-4 **$16.95**

Silence, Simplicity & Solitude: A Complete Guide to Spiritual Retreat at Home
by David A. Cooper 5½ x 8½, 336 pp, Quality PB, 978-1-893361-04-1 **$16.95**

Three Gates to Meditation Practice: A Personal Journey into Sufism, Buddhism, and Judaism
by David A. Cooper 5½ x 8½, 240 pp, Quality PB, 978-1-893361-22-5 **$16.95**

Women Pray: Voices through the Ages, from Many Faiths, Cultures and Traditions
Edited and with Introductions by Monica Furlong
5 x 7¼, 256 pp, Quality PB, 978-1-59473-071-9 **$15.99**
Deluxe HC with ribbon marker, 978-1-893361-25-6 **$19.95**

Spirituality of the Seasons

Autumn: A Spiritual Biography of the Season
Edited by Gary Schmidt and Susan M. Felch; Illustrations by Mary Azarian
Rejoice in autumn as a time of preparation and reflection. Includes Wendell Berry, David James Duncan, Robert Frost, A. Bartlett Giamatti, E. B. White, P. D. James, Julian of Norwich, Garret Keizer, Tracy Kidder, Anne Lamott, May Sarton.
6 x 9, 320 pp, 5 b/w illus., Quality PB, 978-1-59473-118-1 **$18.99**
HC, 978-1-59473-005-4 **$22.99**

Spring: A Spiritual Biography of the Season
Edited by Gary Schmidt and Susan M. Felch; Illustrations by Mary Azarian
Explore the gentle unfurling of spring and reflect on how nature celebrates rebirth and renewal. Includes Jane Kenyon, Lucy Larcom, Harry Thurston, Nathaniel Hawthorne, Noel Perrin, Annie Dillard, Martha Ballard, Barbara Kingsolver, Dorothy Wordsworth, Donald Hall, David Brill, Lionel Basney, Isak Dinesen, Paul Laurence Dunbar. 6 x 9, 352 pp, 6 b/w illus., HC, 978-1-59473-114-3 **$21.99**

Summer: A Spiritual Biography of the Season
Edited by Gary Schmidt and Susan M. Felch; Illustrations by Barry Moser
"A sumptuous banquet.... These selections lift up an exquisite wholeness found within an everyday sophistication." — ★ *Publishers Weekly* starred review
Includes Anne Lamott, Luci Shaw, Ray Bradbury, Richard Selzer, Thomas Lynch, Walt Whitman, Carl Sandburg, Sherman Alexie, Madeleine L'Engle, Jamaica Kincaid.
6 x 9, 304 pp, 5 b/w illus., Quality PB, 978-1-59473-183-9 **$18.99**
HC, 978-1-59473-083-2 **$21.99**

Winter: A Spiritual Biography of the Season
Edited by Gary Schmidt and Susan M. Felch; Illustrations by Barry Moser
"This outstanding anthology features top-flight nature and spirituality writers on the fierce, inexorable season of winter.... Remarkably lively and warm, despite the icy subject." — ★ *Publishers Weekly* starred review
Includes Will Campbell, Rachel Carson, Annie Dillard, Donald Hall, Ron Hansen, Jane Kenyon, Jamaica Kincaid, Barry Lopez, Kathleen Norris, John Updike, E. B. White.
6 x 9, 288 pp, 6 b/w illus., Deluxe PB w/flaps, 978-1-893361-92-8 **$18.95**
HC, 978-1-893361-53-9 **$21.95**

Spirituality / Animal Companions

Blessing the Animals: Prayers and Ceremonies to Celebrate God's Creatures, Wild and Tame *Edited by Lynn L. Caruso* 5 x 7¼, 256 pp, HC, 978-1-59473-145-7 **$19.99**

What Animals Can Teach Us about Spirituality: Inspiring Lessons from Wild and Tame Creatures *by Diana L. Guerrero* 6 x 9, 176 pp, Quality PB, 978-1-893361-84-3 **$16.95**

Spirituality

Awakening the Spirit, Inspiring the Soul
30 Stories of Interspiritual Discovery in the Community of Faiths
Edited by Brother Wayne Teasdale and Martha Howard, MD; Foreword by Joan Borysenko, PhD
Thirty original spiritual mini-autobiographies showcase the varied ways that people come to faith—and what that means—in today's multi-religious world.
6 x 9, 224 pp, HC, 978-1-59473-039-9 **$21.99**

The Alphabet of Paradise: An A–Z of Spirituality for Everyday Life
by Howard Cooper 5 x 7¼, 224 pp, Quality PB, 978-1-893361-80-5 **$16.95**

Creating a Spiritual Retirement: A Guide to the Unseen Possibilities in Our Lives
by Molly Srode 6 x 9, 208 pp, b/w photos, Quality PB, 978-1-59473-050-4 **$14.99**
HC, 978-1-893361-75-1 **$19.95**

Finding Hope: Cultivating God's Gift of a Hopeful Spirit
by Marcia Ford 8 x 8, 200 pp, Quality PB, 978-1-59473-211-9 **$16.99**

The Geography of Faith: Underground Conversations on Religious, Political and Social Change *by Daniel Berrigan and Robert Coles* 6 x 9, 224 pp, Quality PB, 978-1-893361-40-9 **$16.95**

God Within: Our Spiritual Future—As Told by Today's New Adults *Edited by Jon M. Sweeney and the Editors at SkyLight Paths* 6 x 9, 176 pp, Quality PB, 978-1-893361-15-7 **$14.95**

Spirituality & Crafts

The Knitting Way: A Guide to Spiritual Self-Discovery
by Linda Skolnik and Janice MacDaniels
7 x 9, 240 pp, Quality PB, b/w photographs, 978-1-59473-079-5 **$16.99**

The Quilting Path: A Guide to Spiritual Discovery through Fabric, Thread and Kabbalah
by Louise Silk
7 x 9, 192 pp, Quality PB, b/w photographs and illustrations, 978-1-59473-206-5 **$16.99**

The Scrapbooking Journey: A Hands-On Guide to Spiritual Discovery
by Cory Richardson-Lauve; Foreword by Stacy Julian
7 x 9, 176 pp, Quality PB, 8-page full-color insert, plus b/w photographs
978-1-59473-216-4 **$18.99**

Spiritual Practice

Divining the Body: Reclaim the Holiness of Your Physical Self
by Jan Phillips
A practical and inspiring guidebook for connecting the body and soul in spiritual practice. Leads you into a milieu of reverence, mystery and delight, helping you discover your body as a pathway to the Divine.
8 x 8, 256 pp, Quality PB, 978-1-59473-080-1 **$16.99**

Finding Time for the Timeless: Spirituality in the Workweek
by John McQuiston II
Simple, refreshing stories that provide you with examples of how you can refocus and enrich your daily life using prayer or meditation, ritual and other forms of spiritual practice. 5½ x 6¾, 208 pp, HC, 978-1-59473-035-1 **$17.99**

The Gospel of Thomas: A Guidebook for Spiritual Practice
by Ron Miller; Translations by Stevan Davies
An innovative guide to bring a new spiritual classic into daily life.
6 x 9, 160 pp, Quality PB, 978-1-59473-047-4 **$14.99**

Earth, Water, Fire, and Air: Essential Ways of Connecting to Spirit
by Cait Johnson 6 x 9, 224 pp, HC, 978-1-893361-65-2 **$19.95**

Labyrinths from the Outside In: Walking to Spiritual Insight—A Beginner's Guide
by Donna Schaper and Carole Ann Camp
6 x 9, 208 pp, b/w illus. and photos, Quality PB, 978-1-893361-18-8 **$16.95**

Practicing the Sacred Art of Listening: A Guide to Enrich Your Relationships and Kindle Your Spiritual Life—The Listening Center Workshop
by Kay Lindahl 8 x 8, 176 pp, Quality PB, 978-1-893361-85-0 **$16.95**

Releasing the Creative Spirit: Unleash the Creativity in Your Life
by Dan Wakefield 7 x 10, 256 pp, Quality PB, 978-1-893361-36-2 **$16.95**

The Sacred Art of Bowing: Preparing to Practice
by Andi Young 5½ x 8½, 128 pp, b/w illus., Quality PB, 978-1-893361-82-9 **$14.95**

The Sacred Art of Chant: Preparing to Practice
by Ana Hernández 5½ x 8½, 192 pp, Quality PB, 978-1-59473-036-8 **$15.99**

The Sacred Art of Fasting: Preparing to Practice
by Thomas Ryan, CSP 5½ x 8½, 192 pp, Quality PB, 978-1-59473-078-8 **$15.99**

The Sacred Art of Forgiveness: Forgiving Ourselves and Others through God's Grace
by Marcia Ford 8 x 8, 176 pp, Quality PB, 978-1-59473-175-4 **$16.99**

The Sacred Art of Listening: Forty Reflections for Cultivating a Spiritual Practice
by Kay Lindahl; Illustrations by Amy Schnapper
8 x 8, 160 pp, b/w illus., Quality PB, 978-1-893361-44-7 **$16.99**

The Sacred Art of Lovingkindness: Preparing to Practice
by Rabbi Rami Shapiro; Foreword by Marcia Ford
5½ x 8½, 176 pp, Quality PB, 978-1-59473-151-8 **$16.99**

Sacred Speech: A Practical Guide for Keeping Spirit in Your Speech
by Rev. Donna Schaper 6 x 9, 176 pp, Quality PB, 978-1-59473-068-9 **$15.99**
HC, 978-1-893361-74-4 **$21.95**

About SKYLIGHT PATHS Publishing

SkyLight Paths Publishing is creating a place where people of different spiritual traditions come together for challenge and inspiration, a place where we can help each other understand the mystery that lies at the heart of our existence.

Through spirituality, our religious beliefs are increasingly becoming a part of our lives—rather than *apart* from our lives. While many of us may be more interested than ever in spiritual growth, we may be less firmly planted in traditional religion. Yet, we do want to deepen our relationship to the sacred, to learn from our own as well as from other faith traditions, and to practice in new ways.

SkyLight Paths sees both believers and seekers as a community that increasingly transcends traditional boundaries of religion and denomination—people wanting to learn from each other, *walking together, finding the way.*

For your information and convenience, at the back of this book we have provided a list of other SkyLight Paths books you might find interesting and useful. They cover the following subjects:

Buddhism / Zen	Gnosticism	Mysticism
Catholicism	Hinduism /	Poetry
Children's Books	Vedanta	Prayer
Christianity	Inspiration	Religious Etiquette
Comparative	Islam / Sufism	Retirement
Religion	Judaism / Kabbalah /	Spiritual Biography
Current Events	Enneagram	Spiritual Direction
Earth-Based	Meditation	Spirituality
Spirituality	Midrash Fiction	Women's Interest
Global Spiritual	Monasticism	Worship
Perspectives		